CYCLING IN
THE YORKSHIRE DALES

About the Author

Harry has been cycling for as long as he can remember. His first cycle tour was with school friends Graham and Dave across the North York Moors staying in youth hostels during one of those long sunny summers of long ago. After a lengthy break, when the bike was used for commuting, he restarted cycle touring round Ireland then France, Spain, Slovenia and Norway.

Moving to Nidderdale with partner Liz and taking up triathlon were the spur to a new bike, lots more cycling and soon cycling for pleasure took over. Having got the bug again cycling is his preferred method of exercise and foreign travel. He continues to cycle regularly both at home and abroad and pays the bills working as a fitness instructor at the local leisure centre.

Harry has enjoyed re-riding many of his favourite routes and discovering some new ones for this guide and he has no doubt that you will have a great time trying them out.

CYCLING IN THE YORKSHIRE DALES

by Harry Dowdell

2 POLICE SQUARE, MILNTHORPE, CUMBRIA LA7 7PY
www.cicerone.co.uk

© Harry Dowdell 2014
First edition 2014
ISBN: 978 1 85284 687 9

Printed in China on behalf of Latitude Press Ltd.
A catalogue record for this book is available from the British Library.

 This product includes mapping data licensed from Ordnance
Survey® with the permission of the Controller of Her Majesty's
Stationery Office. © Crown copyright 2014. All rights reserved.
Licence number PU100012932

 Base maps by Lovell Johns Ltd www.lovelljohns.co.uk

Acknowledgements

To Liz for your love and ideas, for letting me get on with it, accompanying
me on the routes and modelling for photos on the worst parts of too many
climbs. To John for being a cheerful companion on a number of the longer
rides when the weather should have doused all joy.

Advice to Readers

While every effort is made by our authors to ensure the accuracy of
guidebooks as they go to print, changes can occur during the lifetime of an
edition. If we know of any, there will be an Updates tab on this book's page
on the Cicerone website (www.cicerone.co.uk), so please check before
planning your trip. We also advise that you check information about such
things as transport, accommodation and shops locally. Even rights of way
can be altered over time. We are always grateful for information about
any discrepancies between a guidebook and the facts on the ground, sent
by email to info@cicerone.co.uk or by post to Cicerone, 2 Police Square,
Milnthorpe LA7 7PY, United Kingdom.

Front cover: Approaching Rawthey Bridge, Cautley Crag in the background
(Route 16)

CONTENTS

Overview map 7
Map key 9

INTRODUCTION 11
Geology of the Dales 13
Human habitation 15
Wildlife 17
Getting there and getting about 19
Money 20
When to go 20
Accommodation 22
Food and drink 22
What to wear 24
What to take 25
Choosing your bike 27
Maps 30
Emergencies 31
Using this guide 33

PATELEY BRIDGE 35
Link Route   Leeds Bradford Airport to Askwith 36
Route 1   Nidderdale, Washburn and Wharfedale 38
Route 2   Brimham Moor, Fountains Abbey and Studley Royal 47
Route 3   Masham and Burn Valley 52

GRASSINGTON 58
Route 4   Round Barden 59
Route 5   Malhamdale and High Limestone Country 65
Route 6   Malhamdale by way of Bordley 71
Route 7   Malhamdale, Silverdale and Littondale 75

INGLETON 83
Route 8   Dentdale and round Whernside 84
Route 9   Ribblesdale and round Ingleborough 90

SETTLE 95
Route 10   Dales and Tarn 96
Route 11   Langcliffe Scar and Malham 103

REETH 106
Route 12   Tan Hill 107
Route 13   Wensleydale, Mallerstang and Tan Hill 111
Route 14   Richmond. 125

SEDBERGH 133
Route 15   Lune Valley and Barbondale. 134
Route 16   Circuit of the Howgill Fells 140
Route 17   Barbondale and Holme Open Farm 149

HAWES 153
Route 18   The Big Cheese. 154
Route 19   Semerwater 159
Route 20   Coverdale and Langstrothdale Chase 162

LEYBURN. 171
Link Route   Northallerton to Leyburn 173
Route 21   Swaledale and The Fleak 175
Route 22   Aysgarth Falls 181
Route 23   Jervaulx Abbey and Middleham 185

TOUR DE FRANCE 2014 189
Route 24   Tour de France 2014 Stage 1: Leeds to Harrogate 190

LA VUELTA A DALES 213
Stage 1   Settle to Pateley Bridge 215
Stage 2   Pateley Bridge to Leyburn 222
Stage 3   Leyburn to Hawes 229
Stage 4   Hawes to Muker. 233
Stage 5   Muker to Sedbergh 238
Stage 6   Sedbergh to Settle. 243

Appendix A   Route summary table 248
Appendix B   Useful contacts. 250
Appendix C   Campsites along the Vuelta a Dales 253
Appendix D   Cycles on public transport 256
Appendix E   Basic bike maintenance 259

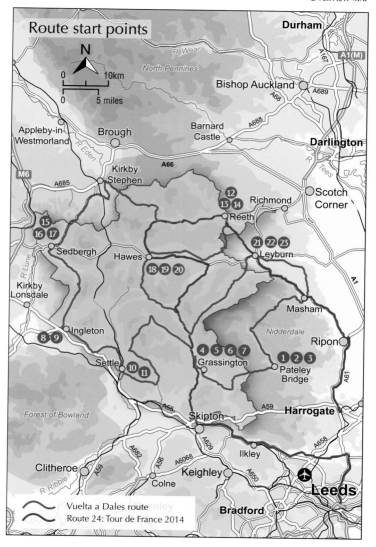

Looking back to Park Rash, Wharfedale (Route 20)

Route symbols on map extracts

 route

alternative route

 Tour de France route

route direction

start/finish point

start point

finish point

alternative start

0   1   2 kilometres
0   1 miles

Features on the overview map

 Vuelta a Dales route

Route 24: Tour de France 2014

Urban area

Yorkshire Dales National Park

Area of Outstanding Natural Beauty

800m
600m
400m
200m
75m
0m

The route maps in this guide are reproduced at 1:100,000 except for those for Route 24 (Tour de France) and the Vuelta a Dales which are at 1:250,000. The town centre maps are based on 1:25,000 OS maps.

GPX files

GPX files for all routes can be downloaded for free at www.cicerone.co.uk/CyclingDales.

Arkengarthdale (Route 12)

Cycling towards Harkerside, Swaledale (Route 21)

INTRODUCTION

A path through the hay meadows, Muker, Swaledale

Ahead the hay meadows were in full flower, similar to those in Asturias, Norway, the Alps and Slovenia, the variety of plants evidence of the poor soil quality. A flagstone path marked the way, linking stiles and field barns. Moulding to the gentle folds of the land it is neither flat nor straight. I've been coming here all my life. I'll be back again.

There is no road in this part of the dale, leaving it to those travelling under their own steam. A wooden footbridge spans the river in its rocky bed. Youthful and lively it babbles, burbles and bickers on its way: once out of the Dales – a landscape born

in water, carved by ice and decorated by man – this spark is lost. Field barns litter the dale, dry stone walls carve it up. The sides are steep, limestone scars breaking through under a fringe of broadleaf trees. The floor is wide and grassy: a classic glacial valley.

The dale bends and the path climbs past long abandoned mine workings. Below the river crashes over Kisdon Force: *foss* and *dal*, Norse words.

Making up the middle section of the Pennines – England's backbone – the Yorkshire Dales is an area of high moorland cut by deep dales. It is home to Britain's most precious landscapes and habitats, a beautiful area of great contrasts with each dale having its own character. Long popular with lovers of the outdoors, in 1954 1769km² of it were designated a National Park.

The visitor travels through small villages set in hay meadows rich in wild flowers. The buildings are made of the underlying stone, the walls standing according to the skills of their builders. Isolated barns wait with empty haylofts, while below there's room for livestock waiting to be gathered in when the season turns. Rising from the dale bottom the steep hillsides are used for grazing. It is a pattern of farming that is seen from the fjords of Norway to the Picos of northern Spain. Here change is slow. Some of the steeper slopes are covered in scree or sparse tree cover. As height is gained the fields increase in size. The gradient eases to reveal extensive plateaus of blanket bog or heather-covered moorland. All too soon the descent starts into the next dale, which is familiar yet distinctly different.

Cyclists enjoy the network of small roads and lanes, some originally built by the Romans while others are upgraded cart tracks or drovers roads. The roads are generally quiet and are used mostly by local traffic. The lack of large urban areas on the fringe keeps the number of visitors low and good trunk roads outside the Dales ensure that heavy traffic has no reason

Drystone walls, Malham

Approaching Dale Head with Pen-y-ghent dominant (Routes 7 and 10)

to pass through. Apart from a small number of quarries there is no heavy industry.

The Yorkshire Dales have hosted visitors for over two millennia and today's visitors will readily find accommodation – camp sites, bunkhouses, Youth Hostels, B&Bs or hotels – and refreshments out in countless pubs, tea shops and restaurants.

GEOLOGY OF THE DALES

The underlying geology, modified by natural and human activities, gives the Dales of today their unique character. Although the pre–Cambrian slates exposed at Thornton Force near Ingleton are the oldest rocks to be found in the Dales it is those deposited during the Carboniferous Period that dominate the landscape. Some

300 million years ago carboniferous limestone was deposited in deep, warm, clear seas. Much of it would have been precipitated but there were also coral reefs, such as that which makes up Skelterton Hill near Cracoe in Wharfedale. As the land periodically encroached on the sea, layers of shale, sandstone, limestone and coal were deposited in the coastal areas. Shale would originally have been deposited as clay or mud some distance from the shore and changed due to the pressure exerted over time by overlying rocks. Sand would have been deposited close to the shore, with tides and currents moving some to form sandy beaches which were subsequently compressed into sandstone. Coal came from trees and other organic matter washed out to sea or deposited in a river bed and then

13

Limestone pavement, Malham Cove

quickly covered so that it did not rot. These rocks are known as the Yoredale facies. Eventually the whole lot was covered by thick deposits of coarse sandstone laid down in huge deltas. This is millstone grit.

Much of the millstone grit and Yoredale facies have been lost leaving carboniferous limestone the dominant rock of the Dales. The Yoredale facies still lay over the limestone of Wensleydale, dominate Swaledale, and make up the higher parts of Pen-y-ghent, Ingleborough and Whernside. The remaining millstone grit can be found forming the high plateaus of boggy moorland of upper Swaledale, Grassington Moor, Barden Moor and Nidderdale as well as capping some of the higher peaks. Subsequent

mineralization of the limestone then deposited ores of lead and barium.

The Carboniferous rocks remain almost horizontal and do not have significant folding but do have some faulting. An area bounded by the Stainmore Trough Fault in the north, the Dent Fault to the West and the Craven Fault to the south was raised relative to the surrounding areas and tilted slightly. This raised area, the Askrigg Block, matches the area commonly defined as the Yorkshire Dales. The line of the Stainmore Fault in the north can be guessed at as the hills drop steeply to the level ground that hosts the A66. The line of the Craven Fault can be clearly seen in the hills that end precipitously parallel to and just north of the A65. The Dent Fault can be followed from Kirkby Stephen to Kirkby Lonsdale along the eastern side of the Howgill Fells, across Dentdale and along the bottom of Barbondale.

The Askrigg Block has been carved by glaciers leaving classic U-shaped valleys separated by high plateaus. Particularly striking are Wharfedale and Swaledale between Muker and Keld. Glacial deposits of boulder clay form the drumlins of upper Ribblesdale and Wensleydale and moraine traps Semerwater and Malham Tarn.

Glacial activity on the limestone has left a karst topography of crags, scars, coves and limestone pavement. This is most striking between Malham and Malham Tarn, the southern part of Whernside, the lower slopes of Ingleborough and much of Wharfedale. Weakly acidic ground water has dissolved limestone giving potholes, sinkholes and extensive cave systems that are popular with potholers.

HUMAN HABITATION

The Dales have been continuously inhabited by mankind since the end of the last ice age, approximately 10,000 years ago. Flints found in caves indicate the presence of Mesolithic people. These were followed by those of the Bronze then Iron Ages who left stone circles and hill forts respectively. Iron Age people lived in small round huts generally located on the limestone plateaus. The Romans occupied the Dales for over 300 years and had a significant fort, Virosidum, near Bainbridge. The Roman road to

Malham Tarn from Capon Hall

Ingleton can still be cycled, albeit by mountain bike, today.

The Dales were then occupied by Angles and Danes who moved up the valleys and also by the Norse who moved in from the west and occupied the upper parts. The villages and hamlets they founded are the villages of today. The ending of a village's names gives an indication of its original settlers. The Angles can lay claim to -ton, -ham, -ley; Danes -by, -thorpe; and the Norse -thwaite, -wick, -sett, -scale. Dale itself derives from *dalr* and fell from *fjall*, both Norse words. Around these villages the land was cultivated and hay harvested while the stock was pastured on higher ground during summer. The hay meadows depend on a nutritionally depleted soil for their rich variety of plants. In the 17th century smallholdings were established

and the fields, small around the villages and larger on the slopes, were walled off. At the same time the field barns were built.

Lead mining has been recorded back to Roman times. It reached its peak in the 18th and 19th centuries. Smallholders would also work as miners. At the same time they made cheese for sale outside the Dales. There were two main methods of getting at the ore. Using the first method, shafts and levels would be dug into a hillside to follow a vein and the ore dug out with the waste material simply tipped nearby. These shafts and levels are easy to find. The second method – hushing – required the vein to run down a hillside. A dam was built above the vein and the vein exposed and then water was released to wash away the remaining soil. Miners then

Gunnerside Gill showing the scars of lead mining

Sheep, a mainstay of Dales farming

worked to loosen the vein while more water accumulated. A grate was placed at the bottom and subsequent flushes washed the heavy ore downhill to be collected by the grate. Waste material filled the valley floors.

The ore was dressed, crushed and mixed with wood or coal, fired and the lead collected. The smoke carried away some lead and so chimneys were built, several hundred metres long, up hillsides. As the smoke cooled the lead was deposited in the soot for later recovery. Spoil heaps, hushes and chimneys along with ruined dressing, crushing and smelting building are significant landscape features, particularly on the north side of Swaledale between Arkengarthdale and Gunnerside Gill. In the early 19th century the population of the

Dales was at its peak. As lead mining declined so did the number of people. Some coal mining was carried out on Fountains Fell and around Greenhow. Today limestone is the only mineral exploited in the Dales.

The post industrial Dales of today depend on the worlds two largest industries: agriculture and tourism.

WILDLIFE

The varied landscape, low-intensity farming and widespread maintenance of traditional practices lead to precious habitats that support a rich variety of wildlife.

The rivers and tarns are home to brown trout almost everywhere. Atlantic salmon return to Ribblesdale, Dentdale and Garsdale to spawn in

Hay meadow, Muker

the gravel river beds. The Bullhead favours firm bottomed, clean and swift shallow water and can be found in Wharfedale, Swaledale, Dentdale, Ribblesdale and Garsdale. White clawed crayfish prefer limestone-rich areas. Healthy fish stocks are enabling otters to recolonise the Dales. In stony stretches of water you should see dippers and grey wagtails while sandpipers and oystercatchers favour rockier shores. The goosander can be found in deeper water and herons can be found everywhere.

Hay meadows managed along traditional lines support a variety of plants including the wood crane's-bill and yellow wagtails are frequent visitors.

The remaining woodland is host to pied flycatchers, wood warblers, green woodpeckers and redstart. Conifer plantations have redpolls, siskins and crossbills. An increasing number of buzzards and red kites now live in the Dales. Owls are common on the woodland fringe but being nocturnal are heard more often than seen. There are roe deer in the woods as well as some of the more exotic escapees from deer parks. The conifer plantations south west of Hawes along with the woods of Mallerstang and Ravenstonedale have populations of red squirrels and there have been many sightings of pine martens. The broadleaved woods are usually made up of ash, wych elm sycamore, oak and birch.

In spring and summer expect to be mobbed by curlews and lapwings protecting their nests on the high pastures and moors. Expect also snipe and redshanks. Hares are a common sight as are rabbits along with their predators, the stoats. You may also come across Highland and Belted Galloway cattle which, unlike sheep, are not fussy grazers and are used to manage the biodiversity of the land. Heather moorland is nearly all managed for shooting red grouse but there are also golden plover and merlin there. Not so common are adders which are quite shy but do enjoy a bit of sunbathing.

Peregrines can be found nesting on some of the remoter crags and Malham Cove is a regular nesting spot for Britain's fastest bird.

GETTING THERE AND GETTING ABOUT

Travelling by car is probably the most convenient way of getting to the Dales. If you are arriving from abroad, you should find a car hire company at, or close to, your point of entry. Making reservations in advance and comparing prices can result in considerable savings. A medium-size five-door hatchback, such as Ford Focus or Renault Megane, will easily take two cycles with the rear seats folded, once the front wheels are removed. See Appendix B for details of car

Gouthwaite and upper Nidderdale before the final steep decent (Route 2)

19

hire companies and agents such as Holiday Autos.

Arrivals at Leeds Bradford Airport, located between Lower Wharfedale and Airedale, face a 10.3km cycle ride to join Route 1 at Askwith. See the Leeds Bradford Airport to Askwith link route before Route 1 for a map and route description.

Less conveniently located but with many more services is Manchester Airport. Cycling from there to the Dales is possible but not a pleasant prospect. First Transpennine Express run trains from the airport to Northallerton. From Northallerton it is a 9km ride to Leeming which is on the Wensleydale Railway or 28.8km to Leyburn. See the Northallerton to Leyburn link route before Route 21 for a map and route description.

Those who wish to use public transport to reach the Dales will find Northallerton a useful starting point. It is well served by a number of train companies most of whom have clearly stated cycle carriage and reservation policies. Many of these companies also service Leeds which has onward connections to the Dales via Northern Rail. However, the cycle carriage policies of Northern Rail do not permit definitive planning. See Appendix D for details of all train companies serving Northallerton and the Dales along with their cycle carriage policies.

Within the Dales there are no known bus services that willingly carry cycles. In reality once you are in the Dales the options are walk, cycle or drive.

MONEY

Cashpoint machines (ATMs) can be found in the larger towns but not all of the villages. In some towns they may only be found in supermarkets, Post Offices or hotels. The majority will not charge for dispensing cash, but many do. At the time of writing, all the main settlements on the routes in this book do have some kind of ATM but the only ones in Summerbridge and Reeth will charge you for withdrawing cash so be warned. (Grassington and Middleham only have one cashpoint each but they are free ones so worth hunting down.)

Cash may be withdrawn over the counter in Post Offices. However not all banks take part in this scheme and some have restrictions as to which accounts can be used. Many shops offer a cashback service.

Visa and MasterCard debit and credit cards are widely accepted, but not universally, accepted and often there is a minimum purchase amount. To be safe ensure you have sufficient cash for whatever you plan to do.

WHEN TO GO

As the seasons turn the Dales offer up something different. Winter has short, often crystal-clear days and a dusting of snow rimming the fells: warm in the sun but sharp in the shadows. Spring brings

Semerwater (Route 19)

the promise of life reborn: trees bud, meadows flower and new born lambs gambol. Warm summer means long days and long rides, when outdoors is the only place to be. Autumn is when the leaves give back their stolen colours, bracken and grasses turn to gold and misty dawns turn to sunny days.

The Dales' weather refuses to play ball with the climate records, and excellent rides are to be had throughout the year. Stable weather systems are all too rare. Weather often turns up in the wrong season and sometimes seasons don't bother turning up at all. Correlation between seasons and the calendar is not good. Cyclists who just go along with the weather, whatever they get, can enjoy cycling all year round.

That said, it would be sensible to expect the most cyclist-friendly conditions from May to September, when average midday temperatures range from 12°C to 17°C and rainfall is generally at its lowest. May is the driest and sunniest month. From October to April the warmth gradually retreats with January and February being the coldest at 4°C. Overnight frosts can be expected from December through to February so watch out for those frozen roads. These temperatures are for the dale bottoms so expect lower figures as height is gained and actual temperatures can vary by up to 10°C from the average for the time of year. The Dales are not the wettest part of Britain, getting around 1500mm of rain annually. Measurable rain is recorded on half of all days, with October to January being the wettest period.

· *Thwaite, Swaledale (Routes 12 and 18)*

Reliable five-day weather forecasts are available online at both www.metoffice.gov.uk and www.bbc.co.uk.

ACCOMMODATION

There is a wide range of accommodation within the Dales, from 'tap and toilet' campsites, through bed and breakfasts to fine country hotels. The National Park and Tourist Information offices listed in Appendix B will be able to provide up-to-date information as to what is available in their area and most offer a booking service.

For the Vuelta a Dales, campsites on or close to the route have been listed. Others can be found at www.ukcampsite.co.uk.

The YHA has five hostels and two camping barns (www.yha.org.uk) in the Dales. Alternatively the independent hostels guide (www.independenthostelguide.co.uk) lists not only hostels but also bunkhouses and bunk barns, which may be of interest to larger groups.

FOOD AND DRINK

A good breakfast is the best way to start a day but you will need more than that to get you through a full day's cycling. Ideally breakfast will include lots of carbohydrates in the form of cereals, porridge, wholemeal bread and fruit. There is nothing wrong with having the bacon and eggs as well.

Short rides, those up to an hour and a half of pedalling time, can generally be completed without extra food. Medium rides, those between one and a half and two and a half hours' pedalling time, will generally require either a snack or a light meal. A snack can include jam sandwiches, bananas or energy bars. A light meal could include a baked potato with cheese, or beans on toast, for example: or the author's favourite of BLT with a portion of chips washed down with a caffè latte. Longer rides will call for a snack and a light meal, or two light meals for even longer ones. Spread the eating through the ride rather than waiting for hunger to strike. Once the ride has finished have something to eat, then go back to your normal daily eating habits.

Keeping water levels balanced is important for good health as water is essential for the body to function correctly. Dehydration – loss of water – thickens the blood and reduces its oxygen-carrying capacity, so reducing performance. Conversely too much water – hyperhydration – dilutes the blood salt concentrations and can be life threatening. At the onset of dehydration the body reacts by turning off urine output and initiates a thirst reaction. The thirst reaction and the body's mechanisms for coping with dehydration may diminish with age. Drink freely to satisfy thirst. Re–hydrating after a long sweaty ride should be considered a whole-day process. Drinking in anticipation of sweat loss can lead to hyperhydration and is best avoided. Coffee and tea may be mild diuretics but one or two cups should have no effect. Water is good for

The Market Place, Masham (Route 24)

Approaching Bordley, Fountains Fell in the Distance (Route 6)

hydration and is readily available but you may prefer a flavoured drink. On the road keep drinks bottles topped up. Drinking at meal times is recommended and generally plain water will be fine. A simple, but not perfect, test of hydration is that urine should be clear and pale straw-coloured, best checked just after you get up in the morning. The author hasn't found specialist drinks and recovery formulations to be necessary, but you may have your own preferences.

Throughout the Dales there are many cafés, tea shops and pubs that readily provide the food and drink cyclists need. For each route café stops are suggested and the pubs included in the route descriptions generally serve food. Cafés that do not display priced menus are best avoided.

WHAT TO WEAR

As the Dales do not have stable weather systems it is recommended that cyclists are prepared for all eventualities. Keep an eye on the weather forecasts to fine tune what to take on each ride. Excess weight and bulk may reduce speed but being cold and wet can be very unpleasant, at best.

- Helmet – Not compulsory but recommended.
- Sunglasses – Reduce glare and keep insects and dust out of eyes. If you have a pair with with interchangeable lenses you can use the non-tinted ones on dark days.
- Cycling top – Short-sleeved cycling tops are great in warm sunny weather.

- Cycling shorts – Cycling shorts with the padded insert are recommended. They can either be figure-hugging Lycra or mountain biker baggy.
- Cycling gloves – Protect hands in case of a fall and to reduce vibrations which lead to sore hands and wrists.
- Shoes – Trainers are fine. Cleated shoes and matching pedals are recommended. Look for cleats that are countersunk into the sole so that walking about is comfortable. Mountain bike shoes are ideal.
- Suntan lotion – Even if it leads to nothing more complex, simple sunburn can be very painful.
- Warm windproof gear – Required to keep warm when stopped and to avoid wind chill when descending. If the weather isn't perfect lots of additional thin layers built up from a thermal base layer are best at keeping out the cold. Running type bottoms, worn over padded cycling shorts, and thermal gloves are welcome additions. Avoid cotton products as they can be very cold when wet.

Cycling in the rain can be cold and unpleasant, and once cold it is hard to get warm again. Consider taking the following:

- Waterproof top – Essential. Ideally breathable to let moisture out, lightweight, brightly coloured and complete with reflective patches. On its own it will be fine for showers.
- Fibre-pile or micro-fleece jacket – Wear under the waterproof top in heavy or driving rain to keep out the cold. Good for retaining warmth when wet and will dry quickly.
- Headwear – A fleece hat or Buff worn under the helmet is really warm.
- Gloves – Waterproof, well insulated gloves are a godsend.
- Trousers – The choice is close knitted cycling trousers which retain the warmth, uncomfortable waterproof trousers, or living with the cold and wet.
- Overshoes – Keep your feet nice and toasty in the worst weather.

WHAT TO TAKE

If you are renting a cycle the hire centre should provide a lock, pump, helmet and repair kit. That is enough for a day ride. If using your own cycle the following may prove useful for day rides.

- Toolkit and spares – See Appendix E for what to take.
- Lock – Although the Dales are relatively crime free it is always worth locking your cycle to an immovable object when left unattended.
- Lights, front and back – If ridden in winter the longer routes will often end at dusk, or in the dark.

Although traffic at those times is very light and it is perfectly possible, if illegal, to ride without lights, it is safer to see and be seen. Even cheap LED lights can be very effective.

- Water bottles – Most cycles have bottle cages fitted or have the lugs to take them. Use these bottle cages and keep the bottles topped up. Hydration backpacks can be very uncomfortable and make the back sweaty. Flavoured drinks can encourage the growth of mould inside the bottle so clean them regularly.
- Bar or saddle bag – Use either a saddle bag or bar bag to hold spare kit, tools and food. A backpack can be uncomfortable and raises the centre of gravity. There is no need to carry more on your back than the clothes you wear. Manufacturers to consider include Ortleib, Carradice and Vaude.
- First aid kit – A small one will do. These are readily available from pharmacists, cycle and outdoor shops.
- Personal items – Spare clothes, money, phone, food, camera etc.

For cycle touring you may also need some or all of the following.

- Camping – Camping is the best way to see a country but increases the load in terms of both weight and volume. Tent, sleeping mat, sleeping bag, stove and cooking utensils can easily add 3kg to 7kg. Food adds more. Panniers, fitted to a solid rack, now become essential. Should more than two panniers be required then seriously reconsider. Camping equipment will add 20–30% to the cycling times given. Equipment can be shared within a group.
- Tents – Most manufacturers make tents suitable for cyclists: generally two-person, easy to erect and lightweight, ranging from 2kg upwards. When travelling solo a mountain marathon tent, which is both smaller and lighter (1kg or under), will suffice. Look for models that have a porch or other storage area for panniers. Manufacturers to consider include Hilleberg, Saunders, Terra Nova, Vango and Vaude.
- Panniers – Manufacturers to consider include Ortleib, Carradice and Vaude. It is always worth putting clothes and other absorbent items inside good quality waterproof bags to guarantee dryness.
- Stoves – Methylated spirits fuelled stoves such as those made by Trangia are well proven, pack down neatly and come complete with a pan set, but can be messy. Gas stoves using re-sealable canisters are lightweight, clean, cook very quickly but require an additional pan set. Manufacturers to consider include MSR and Primus.

All will need some form of ignition: matches for the Trangia and matches or a cigarette lighter for the gas stove. Don't forget a mug, cutlery and cleaning equipment.

- Sleeping gear – A spring, summer or autumn trip means a two or three-season sleeping bag. A silk liner can be added for winter camping, rather than going to the expense of a four-season bag. A good night's sleep is essential for the following day's ride, so take a Therm-a-rest or foam sleeping mat.
- Other items – Use your cycle light as a torch. Unlike hotels campsites generally don't provide soap and towels, so take your own. Lifeventure make light, compact and quick-drying travel towels. As the sun sets the midges come out so some insect repellent may come in useful.

CHOOSING YOUR BIKE

There are no hard-and-fast rules about which type of bike is best for cycling the roads of the Dales. Racing, touring and hybrid bikes are all fine for the rides described in this guide with the exception of the Vuelta for which a more robust touring or hybrid bike may prove to be a better luggage carrier. Mountain bikes are generally heavy and the wide and knobbly tyres make for hard work. However, they do generally have low gear ratios and excellent brakes, which are ideal for the hills: narrow road tyres can be fitted to them. A technical guide on all tyre-related matters, including tyre and rim compatibility, can be downloaded from www.schwalbe.co.uk.

Gears

Having the right gear ratios and using them is important for climbing the

Malham Cove (Route 10)

hills in a state to enjoy the challenge. The gearing required depends on each individual's strength and cardio-vascular fitness, and so the advice that follows is fairly general.

A comparative measure of gearing is how far each full revolution of the pedal moves the bike forward. This is known as 'development' and the development range indicates how suitable a bike is for terrain types and gradients. To calculate the development range, find out the diameter of the wheel in metres, the number of teeth on the largest and smallest cogs on the front chainset and the rear cassette.

Gearing Ratios: The technical bit

- Lower limit of development = π × diameter of wheel × teeth on smallest chainring/teeth on largest ring of cassette

- Upper limit of development = π × diameter of wheel × teeth on largest chainring/teeth on smallest ring of cassette

For a bike fitted with a fairly typical standard chainset with 52 and 32 teeth on the two rings, matched to a cassette with a range of 12 to 25 teeth on its cogs, the development range can be calculated as follows:

- Lower limit = 3.14 × 0.7m × 36/25 = 3.2m
- Upper limit = 3.14 × 0.7m × 52/12 = 9.5m

In the Dales a lower development range of 2.0m to 2.8m is recommended for the steepest climbs. However the author has completed all the routes with a 3.3m lower limit,

Ribblesdale near Stackhouse (Route 10)

Hay meadows, Sedbusk (Routes 13, 18, 19 and 20)

which simply entailed more time out of the saddle. The upper range is less important as long straight descents at high speed are not readily available.

The three most common types of chainset available are (development calculated for a 700mm wheel):

- Standard: Typically 52 and 36 teeth on its two rings and a cassette with a range of 12 to 25 teeth. The development range of 3.2m to 9.5m is ideal for flat and undulating terrain. Standard chainsets are usually found on racing bikes.

- Triple: Typically 52, 39 and 30 teeth on its three rings and a cassette with a range of 12 to 30 teeth. The additional small chainring reduces the lower development distance for a small gain in weight. The development range of 2.2m to 9.5m is very good for the climbs in the Dales. Triples are usually found on hybrid, touring and mountain bikes.

- Compact: Typically 50 and 34 teeth on its two rings and a cassette with a range of 12 to 30 teeth. The smaller chainrings lower the overall development range. The development range of 2.5m to 9.2m is good the climbs in the Dales. Compacts are often available as options on racing and touring bikes.

Within limits it is usually possible to fit different sized chainrings or any chainset type to any bike, either at purchase or as a retrofit. Cassettes can usually be changed for those with different cog sizes relatively easily. If changing chainrings, chainsets or cassettes be aware that the derailleurs may also need changing to cope with the changes in sizes. Your local bike

29

shop will be able to advise on what is possible and will have the correct tools to do the work.

Brakes

Hills in the Dales are often shaped like Christmas puddings; very steep at the bottom with an easing gradient towards a flattish top. This profile can lull the unwary cyclist into an initially rapid descent which accelerates to speeds beyond which brakes remain effective in maintaining control, or which are beyond the expertise of the cyclist.

A twin strategy for descents is required; maintaining control and good brakes. Maintaining control includes descending at speeds that allow stopping within the sightlines; looking ahead for potential hazards such as bends, debris, vehicles, cyclists, wet and broken surfaces; and slowing in anticipation of bends. The type of brake, their setup and the total load will determine stopping distances. The steeper the descent the greater the proportion of weight on the front rather than rear wheel.

Not all brakes are born equal, with weather and wheel type adding complexity. Aluminium wheel rims are generally better for braking than steel, carbon or chrome plated. Rain significantly reduces the effectiveness of brakes that act on wheel rims, but not so much with disc or hub brakes. In the author's experience the effectiveness of brakes in descending order is: hydraulic disc; cable disc; linear-pull or VEE; twin-pivot side-pull; then cantilever. It is important that the brakes work correctly. There should be an even and full application of the pads to the wheel rims or discs without excessive movement of the brake lever and there should be plenty of the brake pads remaining.

Bike hire

The points already discussed relating to bike selection, gear ratios and brake types also apply when hiring a bike. It may not be possible to meet every requirement so expect some compromise. Appendix B lists a number of rental companies along with the types of bikes available. Always check what is included within the bike hire in terms of tools, equipment and so on, as detailed in the 'What to take' section, and find out what to do if there is a major component failure. The cycle should be in good condition: see Appendix E. Those who already have a bike they are happy with might consider taking their own saddle, pedals and bike shoes.

Ensure that the bike is the correct size and check the saddle height, saddle fore–aft position, handlebar reach and handlebar heights are correct. Try out the gears and brakes before leaving.

MAPS

The maps included in this guide should prove more than adequate to navigate the routes. However for those who prefer to do their own thing there are a number of options. Although there are a number of map makers who provide coverage of the Dales, it is the Ordnance Survey who continues to lead the way with a range of reliable and easy-to-read maps.

Those who wish to explore on foot should find the Ordnance Survey 1:25 000 Explorer maps ideal. Most of the National Park is covered by two maps; OL30 *Yorkshire Dales Northern & Central* along with OL2 *Yorkshire Dales Southern & Western*. To cover the routes in this guidebook three more are required: 298 *Nidderdale*, 297 *Lower Wharfedale & Upper Washburn Valley* and OL19 *Howgill Fells and Upper Eden Valley*. These are available as paper maps as well as digitally. Digital suppliers include the likes of TrackLogs (www.tracklogs. co.uk), who can also provide custom maps at various scales. Often included in the bundle is the excellent 1:250 000 OS map of Great Britain. This is a great scale with the right level of detail for long range touring but is no longer available in paper form. All other mapmakers throughout the world should take note.

EMERGENCIES

In a life–threatening emergency:

- firstly ensure that you and the casualty are not in further danger. This may require stopping road traffic, isolating live cables or removing the casualty from a toxic environment;
- then check for response, both physical and audible, and for regular breathing. If unconscious, unresponsive or not breathing

Attermire and Langcliffe Scars (Routes 10 and 11)

Approaching Tan Hill on Long Band (Route 13)

telephone 999 or 112 for help. Chest pain counts as a life-threatening emergency. Give whatever first aid you can;

- telephoning 999 or 112 will get you through to a combined control centre for police, ambulance and the fire brigade. In addition to details of what happened and the casualty's current state they will need to know your location in terms of address or grid reference;

- if back or neck injuries are suspected do not move the casualty unless their life is in danger. Take guidance from the control centre. Being an inconvenience to other road users is not a reason to move a casualty.

The NHS 111 service is available for urgent medical help or advice when the situation is not life-threatening. Telephone 111 if:

- you need medical help fast but it's not a 999 emergency
- you think you need to go to A&E or need another NHS urgent care service
- you don't know who to call or you don't have a personal physician to call, or
- you need health information or reassurance about what to do next.

Where possible, the NHS 111 team will book you an appointment or transfer you directly to the people you need to speak to. If you need an ambulance, one will be sent just as quickly as if you had dialled 999.

Pharmacists can give advice on many ailments.

USING THIS GUIDE

The routes in this book are intended for anyone of at least average fitness and who is fairly confident of their cycling skills on public roads. Those with less experience may need to rest a little more often. The routes are all on roads – with the exceptions of Routes 6 and 14 which have very short unsurfaced sections – and can be ridden on any type of cycle.

Clear, contoured route maps at 1:100,000 (1cm to 1km) and also simple profiles accompany each route description and GPX files are available for every route at www.cicerone.co.uk/CyclingDales. See the back of this guide for full details.

All routes have been graded and have two descriptions.

Long, Medium and Short refer to cycling time, based on distance covered with an allowance for the climb. Cycling time is an estimate of how long the route would take without stopping at an effort equivalent to 25kmph on level ground. (Your own time will vary depending on all the usual factors – experience, fitness, strength, wind and weather.) Stops will add considerably to this.

- Short – up to one and a half hours.
- Medium – up to two and a half hours.
- Long – more than two and a half hours.

Moderate, Hard and Challenging relate to the ratio of total climb to overall distance. There are some challenging climbs on routes described as Moderate or Hard. Note that Easy is not used.

All distances are given in kilometres as recorded on the author's cycle computer. The reader's own measurements will probably diverge as the route proceeds so expect to make some adjustments. The total climb is as measured using a Garmin Forerunner 310XT GPS. For the purposes of this book the accuracy is acceptable although other devices will doubtless give somewhat different results. Where an option or alternative is described the route statistics apply to the option plus the relevant parts of the main route.

Place names are written in bold in the descriptions if they are readily identifiable on the map and the route passes through or close by, to give you an at-a-glance checklist of key waypoints.

The direction 'To' is used where a place is named on a direction sign and the route proceeds directly to that location. For example 'Turn right (19.1km) to Fewston' means the route goes to Fewston by the most direct route from the turn.

The direction 'Towards' is used where a place is named on a signpost but the route does not go there at all, does not go there directly, or there are two named places and only one is on the route. With 'Turn right at the T-junction (52.4km) towards Pateley Bridge and Skyreholme' the route actually goes to Pateley Bridge but passes the turn to Skyreholme. 'Turn' describes what the route does at a junction whereas 'Bend' is what the road does. 'Fork' is used where the turn is oblique.

Barbondale (Route 17)

PATELEY BRIDGE

River Wharfe above Barden Bridge (Route 1)

Pateley Bridge, in Nidderdale, started as a crossing point on the River Nidd between Ripon and Craven. First recorded in the Domesday Survey, it was granted a market charter in the 14th century. It has a full range of services, shops and accommodation, including a modern leisure centre with swimming pool and gym. Pateley retains a livestock market and its agricultural show is held on the third Monday of September. Nidderdale has an industrial history dating back to Roman times, when lead was mined. Quarrying and water-powered mills are evident throughout, but now the only working quarry is at Greenhow. Although most of the mills have been converted into homes some remain as industrial units.

The three routes are largely situated within the Nidderdale Area of Outstanding Natural Beauty (AONB), which stretches from Masham in the north to Ilkley in the south.

PARKING

There are long and short stay car parks on Nidd Walk. There is additional parking in the show ground – which is locked overnight – and on Low Wath Road in the direction of Lofthouse. There is very limited free on road parking in town.

35

LINK ROUTE

Leeds Bradford Airport to Askwith

Start	A685 exit roundabout SE 221 418
Finish	Askwith SE 169 482
Distance	10.3km/6.4 miles
Total climb	115m
Cycling time	40min
Café stops	Otley

This route leads from Leeds Bradford Airport, located between Lower Wharfedale and Airedale, to join Route 1 at Askwith.

Leave the airport terminal and follow the signs for 'all routes'. Continue straight ahead at the roundabout (0.0km) on the A658. Turn right at the T-junction (0.6km) and right again at the next T-junction (1.3km) to East Carlton and Otley. Pass through **East Carlton** and turn left at the T-junction (2.2km) to Otley. Continue straight ahead. Descend and pass Chevin Forest Park.

Bend right, cross over the bypass and enter **Otley**. Turn left at the T-junction (4.6km) towards Pateley Bridge and bend left at Chevin Cycles. In the centre of town bend right then continue straight ahead at the staggered

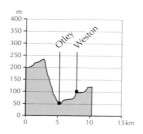

36

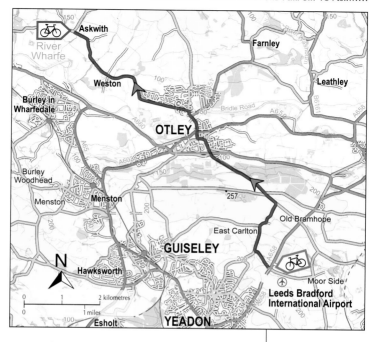

crossroads with traffic lights (5.2km) towards Pateley Bridge. ▶ Bend right then left and cross the River Wharfe. Pass the turn for Pateley Bridge (5.7km). Climb and turn left (5.9km) into Weston Lane to Weston and Askwith. Bend right at the gates, climb round Weston Park – the road levels – and pass through **Weston**. Continue into **Askwith** to join Route 1 (10.3km) at the turn for the village hall.

At these lights Route 24 crosses this Link Route at its 26.9km point.

ROUTE 1

Nidderdale, Washburn and Wharfedale

Start/Finish	Nidd Walk SE 157 655
Distance	65.9km/41.2 miles
Total climb	835m
Grade	Long Hard
Cycling time	3hr 20min
Café stops	Ilkley town centre, Bolton Abbey (Cavendish Pavilion) and Stump Cross Caverns

From Nidderdale the route climbs over to the Washburn Valley and from there into Wharfedale. Much of the route is on narrow lanes with little traffic. The valley roads are rarely level but the more challenging climbs occur when moving from one dale to the next, particularly going from Wharfedale back into Nidderdale.

Turn left, leaving Nidd Walk, and immediately cross the River Nidd. Turn left (0.3km), opposite the Royal Oak, towards the Bewerley Park Centre. There are a couple of sharp but short climbs. Pass through **Bewerley**, turn left (1.2km) and pass the Bewerley Park Centre. Continue on this narrow road as it descends to re-cross the Nidd followed by a steep climb through **Glasshouses**. Turn right at the crossroads (3.2km) towards Knaresborough. Pass through **Wilsill**, descend and pass through **Low Laithe** and continue into **Summerbridge**. Turn right (7.0km) at the Flying Dutchman towards Dacre and Otley.

Descend steeply, re-cross the Nidd and climb through **Dacre Banks**, after which the road steepens considerably. Pass the first right turn in **Dacre** (8.9km) for Braithwaite but take the second right turn (9.3km) towards **Thornthwaite**. Turn right at the T-junction (11.4km) towards Blubberhouses then turn left (11.6km) into Day Lane towards Blubberhouses and Otley, for a

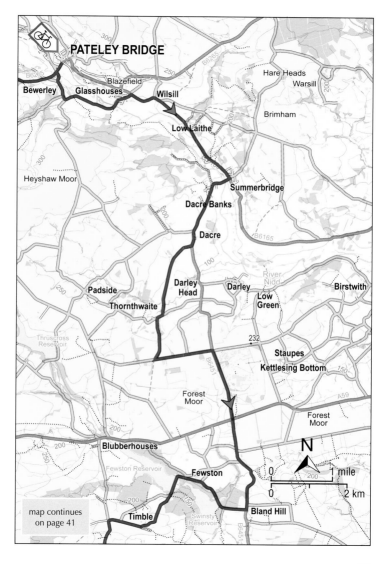

PATELEY BRIDGE

Bewerley Glasshouses Blazefield Wilsill

Hare Heads Warsill

Low Laithe

Brimham

Heyshaw Moor

Summerbridge

Dacre Banks

Dacre

River Nidd

Padside Darley Head Darley Low Green Birstwith

Thornthwaite

Thruscross Reservoir

232

Staupes

Kettlesing Bottom

Forest Moor

A59

Forest Moor

Blubberhouses

Fewston Reservoir

N

0   1 mile

0   2 km

Fewston

Swinsty Reservoir

Bland Hill

map continues on page 41

Timble

39

climb straight up the dale side. Turn left at the T-junction at the top (12.8km) towards Otley, then turn right at the staggered crossroads (14.3km) towards Otley. Pass RAF Menwith Hill. Continue straight ahead at the crossroads with the A59 (16.3km) towards Fewston.

The A59 follows the course of a **Roman road** and by looking right its traces can be seen climbing over Blubberhouses Moor and Round Hill.

The route enters the catchment of the **Washburn**. The Washburn is held back by four reservoirs and much of the moor, woods and farmland is owned by Yorkshire Water (YW). YW have done a lot to open up their land to the public with extra paths and bridleways, picnic areas, car parks and toilets. The upper reservoir, Thruscross, contains the

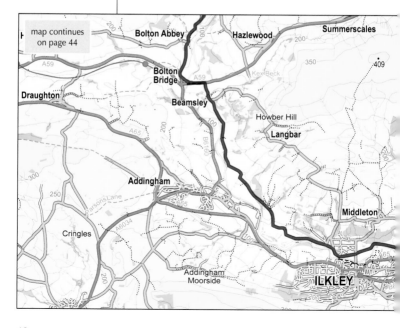

map continues on page 44

submerged remains of West End which can only be visited in time of drought. Controlled releases from Thruscross are popular with kayakers.

Continue and pass the Sun Inn. Turn right (19.1km) to **Fewston**, descend and bend right. Cross a bay of Swinsty Reservoir and climb through the woods. Pass Fewston church, which hosts the Washburn Heritage Centre. Descend and bend left to cross the Fewston reservoir dam. Fork left (21.9km) at the Millennium Stone outside the entrance to the car park and toilets. Climb on this narrow road and pass through **Timble**. Turn left at the T-junction (23.8km), in effect straight ahead. Turn left (24.1km) at the cross roads heading south. The steep climb ends on heather-clad **Askwith Moor**. The views ahead are into West Yorkshire and to the left is the lower

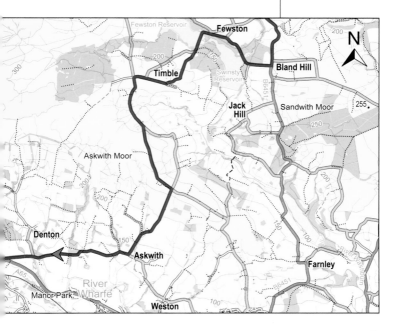

Washburn. Turn right at the crossroads (27.6km) to Askwith and Ilkley and so enter Wharfedale.

Descend with a couple of tight bends into **Askwith** and turn right at the T-junction (29.8km) towards Denton and Ilkley. This undulating and twisty valley road is very popular with local cyclists so expect company. As the road closes on the river it levels off, a rare thing in the Dales. Pass Denton Bridge (33.1km). Enter **Ilkley** and pass the lido. Continue straight ahead at the staggered crossroads (35.3km) to Nesfield and Beamsley. ◄ Bend right then turn left (36.0km) into Nesfield Road. Pass through Ilkley Golf Course, where the road narrows.

A left turn would lead into the centre of Ilkley and tea shops.

The road is twisty with many blind corners, short but steep climbs and descents. Great cycling with snatched views across the dale. Pass through Nesfield and **Beamsley**. Turn left at the T-junction with the A59 (42.5km). After 200m cross the road at the traffic island and take the surfaced bridleway signed B6160, cross the Wharfe and turn right at the T-junction (43.2km). Pass the hotel, arch and **Bolton Abbey**. Turn right (44.9km) by the memorial, signed to the Sandholme car park. Descend through the grounds of Bolton Abbey and pass the car park pay booth to arrive at **Cavendish Pavilion**. Dismount and push your cycle.

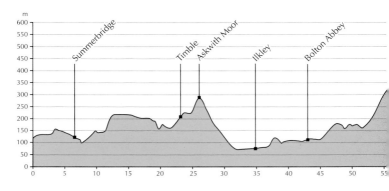

Footbridge and stepping stones at Bolton Priory

Cavendish Pavilion has been a popular stop for cyclists for many years. The basic requirements of café and toilets are met. It is a great location and with some rewarding riverside walks. Upstream is the Strid, a broiling cataract where the Wharfe is squeezed into a narrow channel. Downstream are the ruins of Bolton Priory, an Augustinian priory founded in 1154. The estate is managed by the Chatsworth Settlement Trustees.

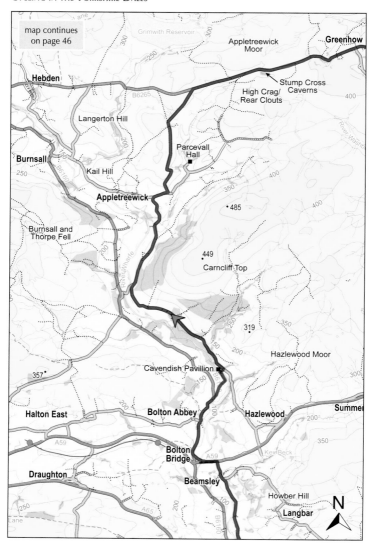

map continues on page 46

Cross the wooden bridge in front of the pavilion and climb the gentle slope to the public road. Turn left at the T-junction (46.0km). The tree shaded road is narrow with some short but steep climbs. Turn right at the T-junction (49.8km) and continue along the undulating side of the dale. Turn right at the T-junction (52.4km) towards Pateley Bridge and Skyreholme. The climb is gentle at first but steepens considerably as it bends left (52.9km). Pass the turn for Skyreholme and Parcevall Hall at this point. ▶

The steep climb does not last forever. To the right and far below is Trollers Gill, which is best approached on foot from near Parcevall Hall. Turn right at the T-junction (56.2km) with the main road to Greenhow and Pateley Bridge. This section can be busy with fast traffic. After a level section climb past **Stump Cross Caverns**. Continue upwards to **Greenhow**, pass straight through the village. Climb past the limestone quarries on the right. The road is lofty and the views of upper Nidderdale quite extensive.

To visit the 24 acres of recently renovated gardens, the largest in the National Park, of Parcevall Hall simply follow the signs.

Nidderdale on a crisp autumn morning

45

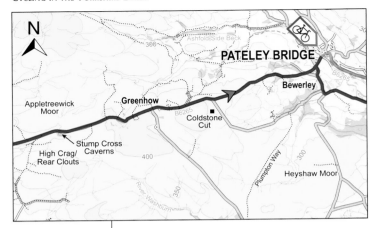

Stump Cross Caverns are limestone show caves open to the public. Remains of reindeer, wolves, bison and wolverine have been found. At over 400m Greenhow is one of Yorkshire highest settlements and it is claimed that St. Mary's is the highest parish church in England.

There is strong evidence that the Romans mined lead here, probably with slave labour. Lead ingots dated to AD81 have been found. At Toft Gate there is a signed path to the viewing platform of **Coldstone Cut**. The platform is an attraction on its own never mind the views of Nidderdale and beyond.

Pass the Toft Gate Lime Kiln and car park (62.5km). The descent into **Pateley Bridge** is often steep with some tight corners so take care. Not everyone gets down unscathed. Enter Pateley and return to the start.

ROUTE 2

Brimham Moor, Fountains Abbey and Studley Royal

Start/Finish	Nidd Walk SE 157 655
Distance	44.5km/27.8 miles
Total climb	575m
Grade	Medium Hard
Cycling time	2hr 15min
Café stops	Studley Royal located close to the lake and in Ripon the market square and close to the cathedral

The route visits three National Trust properties: the Site of Special Scientific Interest (SSSI) of Brimham Moor, with sculpted gritstone tors and heather-covered blanket bog; the World Heritage Site of Fountains Abbey; and the landscaped deer park of Studley Royal. Only Fountains has an entry charge. The route then explores lower Dales country with views across the Vale of York to the North York Moors. The return to Pateley is across high heather-covered moorland and ends with excellent views of Nidderdale.

The route initially follows the Way of the Roses Coast to Coast cycle route 688. Signage is excellent, thus simplifying navigation, so keep an eye open for the blue signs.

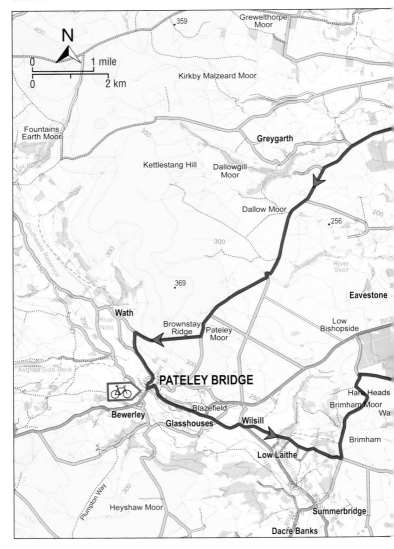

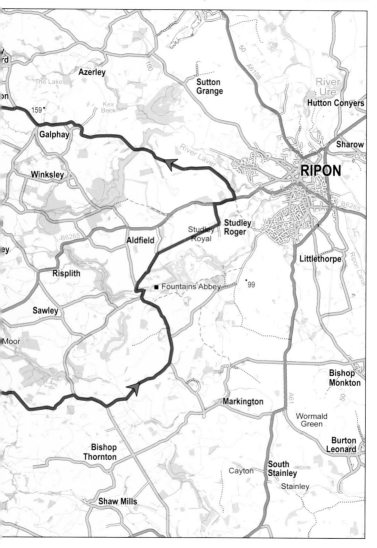

Turn right, leaving Nidd Walk. Climb up the High Street, bend right at the top and stay on this road as it leaves town and continues upward. Pass the turn for Ripon (1.9km), descend through **Glasshouses** and on to **Wilsill**. Turn left at the far side of Wilsill (3.1km) to Smelthouses. ◄ Pass through Smelthouses, climb the three leg-burning sections to Brimham crossroads and turn left (5.9km) towards Ripon. Pass the entrance to the National Trust car park and cross **Brimham Moor**.

The signs can be obscured by vegetation.

> The rocks visible from the road are only a taster for those further west which are accessible from the car park. Water, ice and wind have carved the **millstone grit** into fantastic shapes, many of which have names.

Turn right (8.7km) towards Warsill and keep on this road to the end. Turn right at the T-junction (13.2km) and then next left (14.2km). Pass How Hill – beyond which the ruins of **Fountains Abbey** rise out of the wooded valley – and cross the River Skell (18.7km). Climb then turn right (19.1km) to Fountains Abbey and Studley Royal.

At the roundabout take first exit, signed 'Exit'. Turn right at the obelisk (20.2km) and pass thought the gate into the deer park. Pass the church and continue on this road as it descends. Ripon Cathedral is straight ahead. Pass through the arch and exit the deer park.

> **Fountains Abbey** was founded by Cistercians in 1132 and lasted until 1539, at the Dissolution of the Monasteries. During its time it owned vast estates throughout North Yorkshire and its name still lives on in many places, including a hill on the Pennine Way and a primary school in Lofthouse. Along with Studley Royal, its well preserved ruins are designated a UNESCO World Heritage Site.
>
> Studley Royal is a medieval deer park with Red, Fallow and Sika deer. Landscaping began in 1718 and contains an impressive and recently renovated water garden.

Fountains Abbey

Bend left and pass through **Studley Roger**. Turn right at the T-junction (22.6km) towards Ripon then turn left (23.2km) to Galphay, so leaving the Way of the Roses. Pass through **Galphay** (28.4km) and continue towards Kirkby Malzeard. Turn right at the T-junction (29.5km) and left (30.3km) to **Laverton**. Turn left in Laverton (31.2km) towards Pateley Bridge. After a short climb turn right at the T-junction (32.1km), again towards Pateley. The route climbs relentlessly through walled fields before crossing open heather moorland. Cross **Skell Gill** and turn right (38.0km) towards Pateley. Turn right into a narrow lane (40.5km) with an unsigned junction. Descend past disused quarries to the left with excellent views across and up the dale. Turn left (42.3km), descend steeply and turn left again at the T-junction. Continue on this narrow road and return to **Pateley Bridge**.

ROUTE 3
Masham and Burn Valley

Start/Finish	Nidd Walk SE 157 655
Distance	53.9km/33.7 miles
Total climb	715m
Grade	Long Hard
Cycling time	2hr 45min
Café stops	Masham (Bordar House Teas is the cyclists' café) and How Stean Gorge, signed from Lofthouse

Taking in some of the gentler lower dales and lofty heather moorland, the market town of Masham and Burn Valley this ride is popular with the cyclists of Nidderdale. Steep climbs and descents are not forgotten.

Turn right, leaving Nidd Walk. Climb up the High Street, bend right at the top and stay on this road as it leaves town and continues upward. Turn left (1.9km) as the road levels towards Ripon and climb steeply through **Blazefield**, beyond which the gradient eases. Turn left (3.1km) towards Kirkby Malzeard. Climb, descend and climb again. The open moorland starts at Skell Gill. Leave

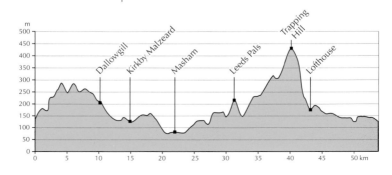

the moor (10.1km) and descend. Turn left (12.6km) to Kirkby Malzeard. In **Laverton** cross the river and turn left at the T-junction (13.4km) to Kirkby Malzeard and Masham. Climb then descend into **Kirkby Malzeard**. Turn left (15.0km) to Grewelthorpe and Masham. Follow this hedged lane and turn right (17.1km) into **Grewelthorpe**. Climb over the small rise and turn left at the T-junction in front of the Crown Inn. Bend right and leave the village. Pass Hackfall Woods on the right.

River Ure, Hackfall Woods

> **Hackfall Woods** are a Grade 1 Listed Landscape Garden and SSSI. Landscaping of this 100m gorge overlooking the River Ure started in 1765. The semi-natural woodland has recently been restored and is home a wide variety of trees, plants and birds. The woods can be accessed from Grewelthorpe and along the road towards Masham. A heartily recommended diversion for which there is no charge.

Climb then descend past Roomer and across Nutwith Common. The descent continues almost to Masham. Enter **Masham** and note the turn (22.1km) for Swinton and Ilton. Bend then turn right into the market place (22.4km). ▶

Stock up here as there really isn't anything until Lofthouse and even there it can be very limited or shut.

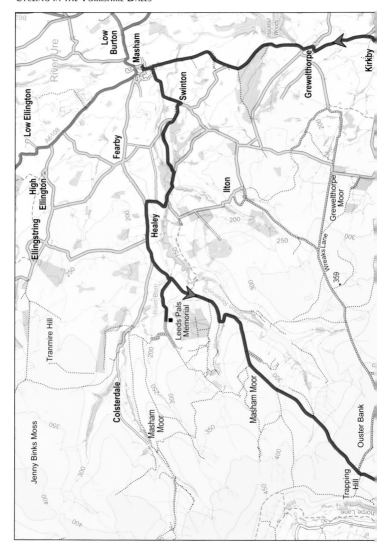

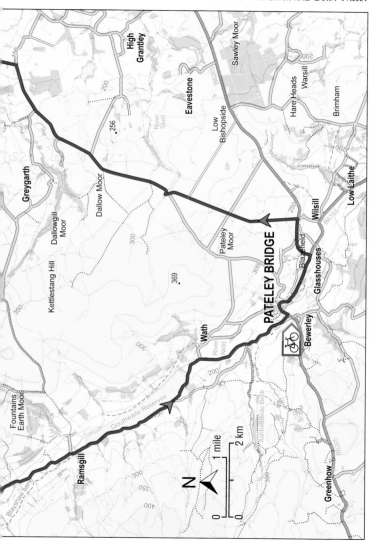

55

Masham lays claim to the largest market square in Yorkshire, the market charter dating back to 1250. It has two breweries, each with its own visitor centre. Importantly for us it has a good range of shops, pubs and cafés. For those who seek a little action the town hosts a Stream Fair and Organ Rally on the third full weekend of July and in late September there is the sheep fair. Sadly use of the market square as a car park reduces its charm considerably.

Retrace the route and turn right (22.7km) towards Swinton and Ilton. Pass the golf club, cross the River Burn and climb. Turn right (24.1km) in front of Swinton Park and pass through the village of **Swinton**. The route repeatedly changes sides of the valley to add to the climb. Beyond the grounds of Swinton Park descend and ford the beck (26.7km). There is also a footbridge. Turn right (27.2km), cross the river and climb to Healey. Turn left at the T-junction (28.0km) by the school to Healey and Lofthouse. ◄ Pass through **Healey**. Pass the turn (29.6km) for Colsterdale. Descend and cross the river. Turn right (30.3km) to the **Leeds Pals Memorial**. Climb to the memorial and take in the view.

The sign may be hidden in the hedge.

The **Leeds Pals** were the 15th Battalion of the West Yorkshire Regiment. Recruited from the crowded and heavily polluted city of Leeds in September 1914, they decamped here for training. For many it would be the best time of their lives.

In December 1915 they served on the Suez Canal. In summer of 1916 they moved to France for the Battle of the Somme. Within minutes of Zero Hour, 0730, on the first day of battle there were 528 casualties, of whom 248 lay dead. Not one inch of ground was taken. Of the 900 Leeds Pals who fought at the Somme 750 were killed.

Retrace the route to the main road and turn right at the T-junction (32.6km). Climb and prepare to climb more. Dry stone walls soon replace hedges. Pass **Leighton**

Lofthouse, Nidderdale

Reservoir. Climb past Pott Hall and pass between the 'Unsuitable for goods vehicles and buses' signs (36.1km). Cross unenclosed heather-covered Masham Moor, descend to cross a stream and climb again to the cattle grid at 429m (40.1km). There are good views of upper Nidderdale including Great and Little Whernsides. The descent into Lofthouse is often very steep and twisting on a road that barely manages to hold on to the hillside itself. Fortunately the walls are high and obliterate the views that would otherwise distract. Pass the farm selling its own ice cream and enter **Lofthouse**. Pass the Crown Hotel. Turn left at the T-junction (43.3km) to Pateley Bridge and keep on this road as it undulates its way along the valley bottom.

> **To visit the top end of Nidderdale** turn right at the T-junction in Lofthouse and after 200m right again onto the Yorkshire Water access road. The road over-lies the old railway track bed built for the construction of Scar House and Angram reservoirs. The climb is constant but good going. Cyclists are permitted through the top gate up to Angram reservoir wall.

Pass through **Ramsgill**, with the Yorke Arms, then alongside **Gouthwaite Reservoir**. Pass Wath and return to **Pateley Bridge**. Turn left at the T-junction next to the petrol station to return to the start.

GRASSINGTON

Burnsall, Wharfedale (Routes 4 and 7)

Perched on a ledge above the River Wharfe, Grassington is surrounded by a limestone landscape. The town centre is picturesque and attracts many visitors. It gained its Royal Charter in 1282 but it wasn't until the 17th to 19th centuries, when lead mining was at its peak, did the town start to prosper. The arrival of the railway in Threshfield really started the tourist business which, along with farming and quarrying, remains the economic mainstay of the area. The River Wharfe starts life in narrow Langstrothdale and enters Wharfedale at Hubberholme, where the valley widens. It is not until well downstream of Grassington that it leaves the classic limestone country of crags and scars marked hills.

Malham is attractive in its own right but most visitors, including many students on field trips, come to see the geological features. Malham cove is an 80m sheer curved cliff. Malham beck emerges at the bottom while at the top a prime example of limestone pavement provides microclimates for lime loving plants. Peregrine falcons can be seen nesting near the top. Gordale Scar is a 100m deep ravine with a couple of waterfalls. Janet's Foss is a small and beautifully set waterfall. Malham Tarn is England's highest lake. The water is trapped by glacial deposits and its distinctly alkaline chemistry is very rare.

PARKING

There is a large car park at the National Park Visitor Centre on the Pateley Bridge road a short distance from the centre of town. On road parking is very limited.

ROUTE 4
Round Barden

Start/Finish	Grassington National Park Centre SE 002 638
Distance	41.3km/25.8 miles
Total climb	455m
Grade	Medium Moderate
Cycling time	2hr
Café stops	Hebden, Bolton Abbey (Cavendish Pavilion), Embsay railway station and Cracoe

This route circumnavigates the group of fells collectively known as Barden Moor. In doing so it progresses from limestone to millstone grit and back again. As it does so the nature of the ride also changes.

Turn right leaving the visitor centre and down the dale away from town. In **Hebden** turn right (2.5km) towards Burnsall immediately before the bridge on the main road. Pass through the village and descend towards the Wharfe on a narrow and twisty road that can be quite dirty. The views are good, including those overlooking Burnsall. Turn right and downhill at the T-junction (5.1km) to Appletreewick. Turn left at the T-junction

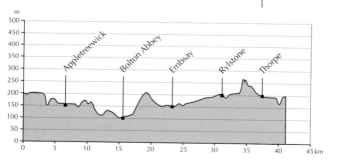

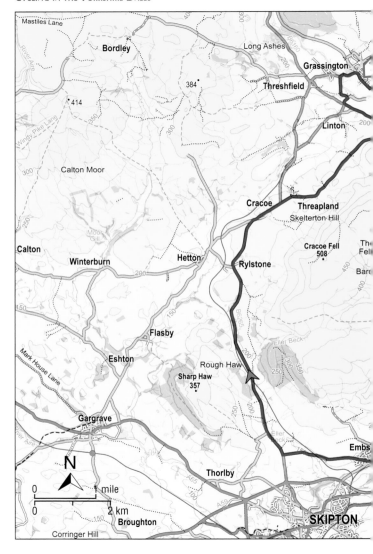

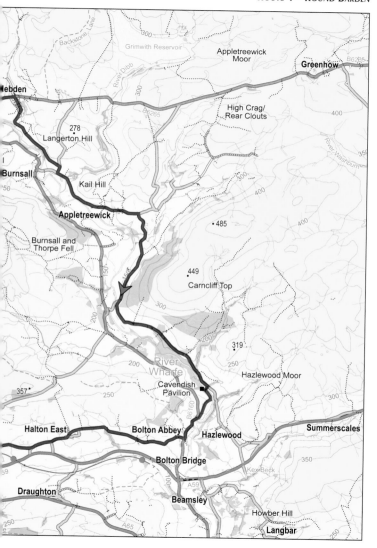

(5.3km), again to Appletreewick. The narrow undulating road to Appletreewick has good views of the river. Pass through **Appletreewick**, with its two fine pubs. Turn right (7.9km) towards Barden and Bolton Abbey down the valley. Turn left (10.6km) towards Hazlewood and Storiths on a narrow lane. The road passes through woodland and has a few steep ups and downs. Turn right (14.3km) at the unsigned crossroads, dismount and cross the bridge to **Cavendish Pavilion**.

> **Cavendish Pavilion** has been a popular stop for cyclists for many years. The basic requirements of café and toilets are met. It is a great location and with some rewarding riverside walks. Upstream is the Strid, a broiling cataract where the Wharfe is squeezed into a narrow channel. Downstream are the ruins of Bolton Priory, an Augustinian priory founded in 1154. The estate is managed by the Chatsworth Settlement Trustees.

Bolton Priory, stepping stones optional

Turn left towards the car park before remounting and take the access road uphill and out of the parkland. Turn

left at the T-junction (15.4km) by the monument. ▶ Pass through **Bolton Abbey** and under the arch. Turn right (16.1km) at the small green towards Hesketh Park Farm. The road climbs gradually to Halton East, firstly as a walled lane but as height is gained through open pasture. Pass through **Halton East** (19.5km), with the telephone box and white cottage to the right, towards Embsay and Skipton. Continue straight ahead at the first and second (20.6km) turns. A quarry dominates the skyline to the left while the valley bottom hosts the Embsay and Bolton Abbey Steam Railway. Enter **Embsay** and immediately turn left (22.5km) towards Skipton and left again at the T-junction (23.0km).

There are good views of the priory to the left.

> **Embsay** is a largely Victorian town and terminus on the Embsay and Bolton Abbey Steam Railway. The other terminus, needless to say, is at Bolton Abbey. Cycles are carried for free in the guard's van, should you wish to go multimodal.

Pass the railway station and turn right (23.6km) into Brackenley Lane. There is a very short section of cobbles at the town boundary. Continue on this narrow lane, pass under the railway and climb to the main road. Turn right at the T-junction (25.9km). For the Dales this road is reasonably busy but there is still time to take in the views of Flasby Fell to the west and Embsay Moor, Rylstone and Cracoe Fells to the east. Pass through **Rylstone** (31.3km) and on to **Cracoe**.

> It was the **Rylstone and District Women's Institute**'s saucy fundraising calendar that inspired the makers of the film *Calendar Girls* and so many other voluntary groups and businesses to do the same. Not so widely copied was turning the village green into a duck pond.

Turn right at the far end of Cracoe (33.8km) onto a narrow lane with blue Way of the Roses markers. Bend right and climb. The lane is narrow with plenty of twists, turns, ups and downs. Walled lanes don't come any better.

There are views across Wharfedale with Grassington, Grass Wood and Kilnsey Crag all discernable. Pass round Elbolton Hill and turn left at the T-junction (37.7km) on the edge of **Thorpe**.

> The rounded **hills around Thorpe** are relict limestone reefs. Tucked away in one of the hollows the hidden village of Thorp was missed by the marauding Scots in the 14th and 15th centuries. Nearby **Elbolton Cave** has yielded Neolithic and Bronze age pottery as well as bones of reindeer, arctic foxes, brown bears and wolves.

Descend to the main road and turn left at the T-junction (38.4km) towards Threshfield. Turn right at the crossroads (39.7km) towards Linton falls. Bend left, pass the school and turn right at the T-junction (41.0km). Cross the river and climb into **Grassington**. Follow the road as it bends right to return to the start.

ROUTE 5

Malhamdale and High Limestone Country

Start/Finish	Grassington National Park Centre SE 002 638
Distance	49.4km/30.9 miles
Total climb	710m
Grade	Long Hard
Cycling time	2hr 35min
Café stops	Cracoe and Malham (The Old Barn on the main road and Beck Hall signed off Cove Road)

For many Malham epitomises the Yorkshire Dales. A delightfully pretty stone built village surrounded by a stunning limestone landscape. This clockwise route starts pleasantly enough but as Malham nears the scenery gets better and better. After a sharp climb out of the village the landscape changes to dry valleys, pavement and crags. The return down Littondale and Wharfedale tops off the ride.

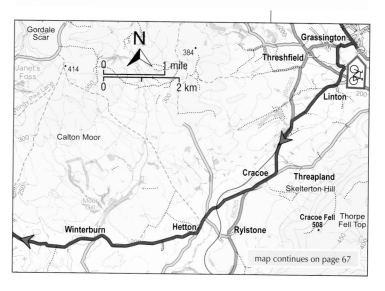

map continues on page 67

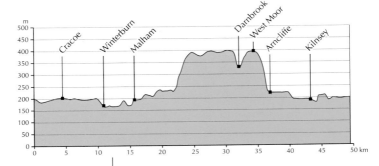

Turn left, leaving the visitor centre. Bend left in town, descend and cross the Wharfe. Immediately turn left (0.7km) to Linton. Bend right, climb and continue straight ahead at the staggered crossroads (1.4km). Pass through **Linton**.

> **Linton Falls** is caused by the North Craven Fault and is the site of a recently installed hydroelectric power plant. Linton itself is a picturesque village with a shady green.

Turn left at the T-junction (3.5km). Pass through **Cracoe**. Turn right (6.0km) at the far end of the village to Hetton. The next few kilometres are on quiet, twisty, undulating roads though attractive lush pasture. In **Hetton** turn right (7.9km) to Winterburn and Airton. Pass through **Winterburn** and turn right (10.9km) over a small bridge to Airton and Malham. In **Calton** bend left (14.0km), descend and cross the Aire. Climb to **Airton** village green. Keep right and turn right at the T-junction (14.7km) onto the main road heading north. Pass through **Kirkby Malham** (16.7km). ◄ The road climbs and from the top Malham Cove and Gordale can be seen ahead. Descend and enter **Malham**.

St Michael's Church next to the Victoria Inn is worth a quick look.

> For more information on **Malham** see the introduction to this chapter.

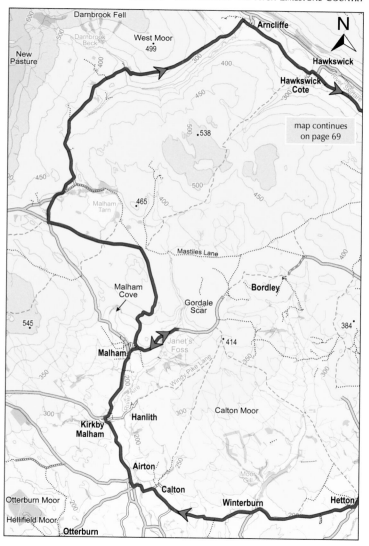

map continues on page 69

Limestone pavement, Malham Cove

Turn right (18.8km) over the bridge to Gordale. Pass the Youth Hostel, where a path leads to Malham Cove. Pass, but note the left turn (19.1km). Climb and descend to Gordale Bridge. At the bottom of the descent is a path to **Janet's Foss** and just beyond the bridge is a footpath through the campsite to **Gordale Scar**. There are plenty of road signs for locking cycles to.

Having done the sights return towards Malham. Turn right (21.6km) towards **Malham Tarn** for a challenging climb out of the dale. On a sharp right bend (22.6km) a footpath leads to the top of Malham Cove, with its limestone pavement and giddy views. The steep climb continues in a shallow dry valley but the gradient eventually eases. Bend left (25.0km) towards Settle and gently descend to pass the outflow of Malham Tarn. Turn right at the crossroads (27.6km) and right again at the T-junction (28.2km) to Arncliffe.

Much of the next section is above 375m which is great in summer sun but can be bleak and inhospitable in wind and rain. The pasture is lush and the scenery spectacular.

◀ Descend steeply into and out of Darnbrook. Limestone scars and pavement are the dominant features

68

on the hillside opposite. After prolonged rain water spurts out of the hillside in a line of springs and spouts. The descent into Arncliffe is very steep in places. The views of Littondale improve as height is lost.

Cross the river (36.7km) and enter **Arncliffe**. Pass the Falcon Inn on the village green and turn right at the T-junction (37.1km), in effect straight ahead. Continue down the valley and turn right at the T-junction (42.1km)

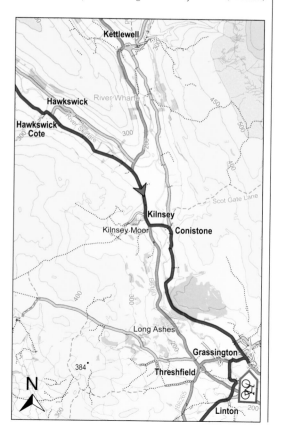

Looking back at Yew Cogar Scar approaching Littondale

towards Settle and Grassington. Pass under Kilnsey Crag and through **Kilnsey**. Turn left (43.7km) to **Conistone** and cross the River Wharfe. Bend right (44.2km) in Conistone to Grassington. Continue on this road all the way back to Grassington as it wends its way passing below Grass Wood as it does so.

> **Kilnsey Crag**, a 50m cliff with a 10m overhang, attracts rock climbers by the score. Grass Wood is ancient woodland which has been designated a SSSI for its woodland flowers. The underlying limestone is present as outcrops, scars, scree and pavement so providing a wide range of habitats.

Enter **Grassington** and turn left at the T-junction (49.0km) towards Hebden and Pateley Bridge to return to the Visitor Centre.

ROUTE 6

Malhamdale by way of Bordley

Start/Finish	Grassington National Park Centre SE 002 638
Distance	32.6km/20.4 miles
Total climb	605m
Grade	Medium Challenging
Cycling time	2hr 5min
Café stops	Malham (The Old Barn on the main road and Beck Hall signed off Cove Road) and Cracoe

Grassington to Malham via Bordley is the shortest route given from Grassington. Payment is a stiff climb and short but rideable off road section. Bordley to Lee Gate, some 2km, includes a mixture of farm tracks and pasture. The author has ridden it on his racing cycle with skinny wheels and tyres without difficulty, although some may wish to push the odd section. The descent to Malham is worth the effort.

Turn left leaving the visitor centre. Bend left in town, descend, cross the River Wharfe and continue uphill. Turn right at the T-junction (1.6km) towards Kilnsey then turn left (1.8km) to Skirethorns. Pass through **Skirethorns**, where the climb starts. Turn right at the crossroads (2.8km) to Malham, signed 'unsuitable for motor vehicles'. The climb alternates between steep and steeper on a road hemmed in by dry stone walls and shaded by a good scattering of trees. As height is

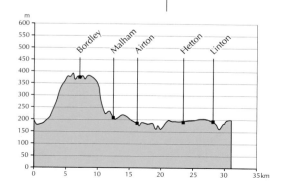

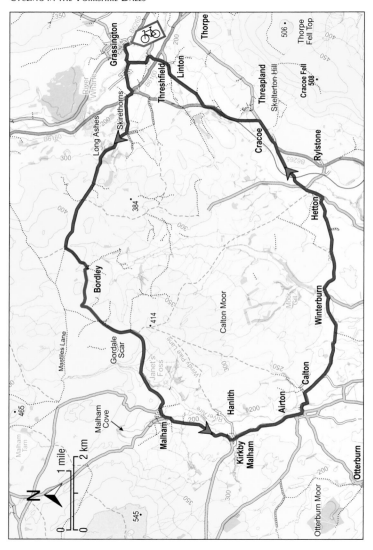

gained the trees disappear, the gradient eases and lime-stone pasture takes over. Outcrops of limestone break through on either side.

Cross the cattle grid (6.1km) into unenclosed big sky pasture and continue ahead. After a short descent pass through the gate (6.6km) and immediately turn left through a second. A wood finger post points to Bordley. Climb the rough road and descend on the asphalt farm road. Prepare to stop for the gate. Pass through **Bordley** with the farmhouse on the right, then with the stone barn to the left bend right and climb to the metal gate. There should be a right of way sign just past the barn. Pass through the gate (7.6km) and climb on the rough track. As the gradient eases rideability improves. Cows and sheep are usually friendly.

When the rough track fades out (8.4km) follow the faint grass track due west across the field which is about 45° to the wall on the left. Pass through the metal gate (8.6km), bend right and descend into the shallow dry valley. Turn left and climb out on the faint track. ▸ Continue straight ahead when joining the more substantial track from the left (8.9km). Pass through two gates and again continue straight ahead when joining the more substantial track, this time from the right. Descend to Lee Gate farm and at the first building turn sharp right and pass in front of the cottage. Turn left at the T-junction (9.7km) and pass through the gate where the asphalt road begins.

The track does improve.

The descent of Gordale is a delight, narrow and steep in places but with good views over Malhamdale. As height is lost the limestone scars to the right reveal themselves.

Park up by the campsite for a walk into **Gordale Scar**. Cross Gordale Bridge and just ahead is a steep climb. At its bottom (11.9km) a short path leads to the delightful and popular **Janet's Foss**.

After the short climb is a gentle descent into **Malham**.

For more information on **Malham** see the introduction to this chapter.

Descent into Gordale

Turn left at the T-Junction (13.3km) in Malham, towards Settle and Skipton. The road climbs, drops, twists and turns in a delightful rather than malicious way. The scenery will divert your thoughts from any effort. Pass through **Kirkby Malham**. In **Airton** turn left (17.4km) and left again on the village green. Descend and cross the river. Climb to **Calton** and bend right (18.1km) to Winterburn and Hetton. Pass the unsigned right turn (18.7km) and continue on this rollercoaster of a road. Pass over a small bridge and immediately turn left (21.1km) to Hetton and Grassington. Pass through **Winterburn**.

Turn left at the T-junction (24.2km) in **Hetton** towards Cracoe and Grassington. Pass the turns for Rylstone then Bordley. Turn left at the T-junction (26.0km) towards Grassington and pass though **Cracoe**. Continue on this road and bend left beyond the village. Pass the working quarry on the left then turn right (28.5km) to Linton. Pass though **Linton** and continue straight ahead at the staggered crossroads towards Linton Falls. Bend left, pass the school and turn right at the T-junction. Cross the river and climb into **Grassington**. Follow the road as it bends right to return to the Visitor Centre.

ROUTE 7
Malhamdale, Silverdale and Littondale

Start/Finish	Grassington National Park Centre SE 002 638
Distance	71.8km/44.9 miles
Total climb	760m
Grade	Long Moderate
Cycling time	3hr 35min
Café stops	Hebden, Burnsall, Cracoe, Malham (The Old Barn on the main road and Beck Hall signed off Cove Road) and Kettlewell

A ride that has so much: undulating pasture, the spectacle of Malham, the lofty col by Pen-y-ghent, the descent into Littondale, the 'now you see it now you don't' River Skirfare, picture perfect hamlets and villages. The climbs out of Malham and after Sannat Hall Farm can be challenging.

Turn right leaving the visitor centre and down the dale away from town. In **Hebden**, immediately before the bridge on the main road, turn right (2.5km) towards Burnsall. Pass through the village and descend towards the River Wharfe on a narrow and twisty road that can be quite dirty. ▶

The views are good including those overlooking Burnsall.

Turn right and downhill at the T-junction (5.1km) towards Appletreewick. Turn right at the T-junction (5.3km) to Burnsall. Descend, cross the River Wharfe and enter **Burnsall**. Turn right at the T-junction on the green (5.9km) towards Grassington back up the dale.

> **Burnsall** is a charming riverside village sat in a glorious location. The stone buildings have a charm and cohesion and the riverside paths are worth a walk.

Turn left (7.9km) to **Thorpe** and climb steeply to this hamlet tucked away in the folds of the hills.

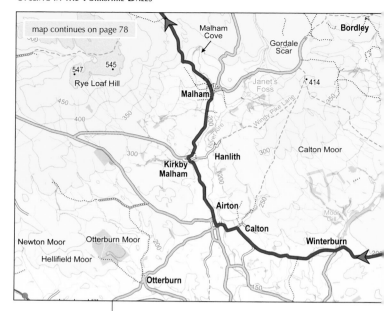

map continues on page 78

The rounded **hills around Thorpe** are relict limestone reefs. Tucked away in one of the hollows the hidden village of Thorp was missed by the marauding Scots in the 14th and 15th centuries. Nearby **Elbolton Cave** has yielded Neolithic and Bronze age pottery as well as bones of reindeer, arctic foxes, brown bears and wolves.

Pass through the hamlet and turn left (8.6km) into a narrow walled lane that swoops and soars along the lower slopes of the Barden fells. Turn left at the T-junction (12.6km) with the main road, in reality straight on, and pass through **Cracoe**. Turn right (13.6km) at the far end of the village to Hetton. The next few kilometres are on quiet, bendy, undulating roads though attractive pasture.

Turn right (15.5km) in **Hetton** to Winterburn and Airton. Pass through **Winterburn** and turn right (18.5km)

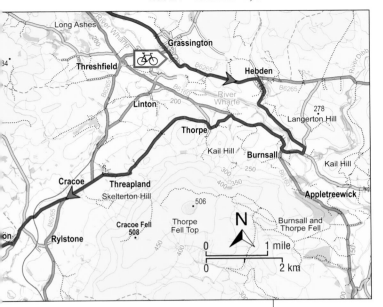

over a small bridge to Airton and Malham. In **Calton** bend left (21.6km), descend and cross the River Aire. Climb to **Airton** village green. Keep right and turn right at the T-junction (22.3km) onto the main road heading north. Pass through **Kirkby Malham** (24.3km). ▶ The road climbs and from the top Malham Cove and Gordale can be seen ahead. Descend and enter **Malham**.

St Michael's Church next to the Victoria Inn is worth a quick look.

> For more information on **Malham** see the introduction to this chapter.

Keep left (26.3km) at the main junction in Malham towards Arncliffe and Malham Tarn. The climb is steep then steepens, with a few sharp bends thrown in to add to the fun. The limestone walls are quite high but the odd gate or stile allow views of Malham Cove to the right. Gradually the gradient eases and the walls reduce giving

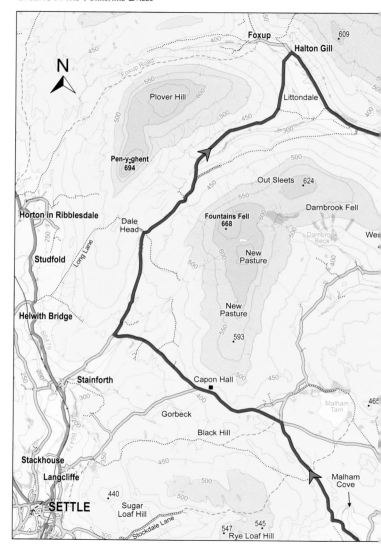

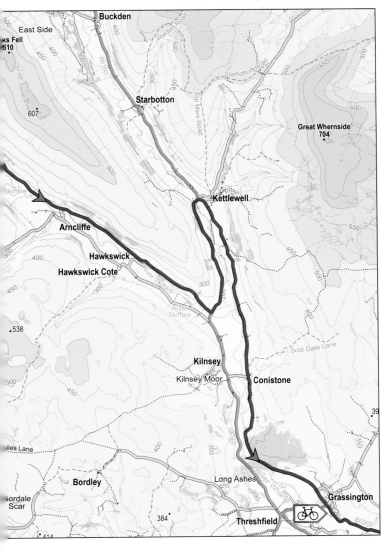

Along Plover Hill with Pen-y-ghent Gill below

views of dry valleys, pavement and craggy bluffs typical of this limestone area.

Turn left at the crossroads (30.7km) towards Langcliffe and Settle. Turn left at the T-junction (31.5km), in effect straight on. Turn right (33.3km) into an unsigned walled lane which descends gently before a vicious down and

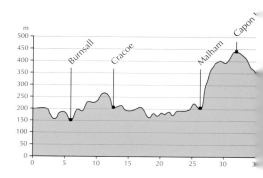

up at Fornah Gill. Turn right at the T-junction (36.0km) by Sannat Hall Farm to Halton Gill. Ahead lies the bulk of Pen-y-ghent with its sharp southern ridge prominent on the left while to the right lies the massive Fountains Fell, the summit of which is hidden by its own slopes.

Halton Gill, Littondale

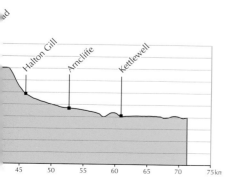

Climb to **Dale Head** before a gentle descent along the flank of Plover Hill. The gradient increases as Halton Gill and Littondale near. There are good long views down the valley. Cross the River Skirfare. Turn right (46.0km) immediately before **Halton Gill**, cross the small stream and continue down the valley towards Litton and Arncliffe.

The floor of the dale is the only level cycling on this route. To the right you may either see the River Skirfare or just its bed, depending on recent rainfall. This is one of those disappearing rivers. Pass through **Litton** (49.4km). Approaching Arncliffe turn left (53.1km) to and through **Hawkswick**. This narrow lane ambles pleasantly down the dale before descending through open pasture. Turn left at the T-junction (58.1km) and climb into Wharfedale. This is probably the narrowest part of this dale but soon Kettlewell and the broad valley reveal themselves.

Descend into **Kettlewell**, cross the River Wharfe and turn right (61.5km) towards Scargill House. Yet another of those narrow walled lanes that amble down the dale with occasional short climbs and sweeping descents. Kilnsey Crag stands out on the other side of the valley. Pass straight through **Conistone** and continue on this road back to Grassington, passing under Grass Wood on the way. In **Grassington** turn left (71.4km) at the T-junction towards Hebden and Pateley Bridge and return to the Visitor Centre.

Crummack Dale overlooking Austwick (Route 9)

Set in a steep-sided valley, where the rivers Doe and Twiss join to become the Greta, Ingleton is popular with walkers, cavers and day trippers. The nearby limestone dales are riddled with holes. In addition it has a seasonal open air heated swimming pool for a post-ride dip. The big draw is the Ingleton Waterfalls Trail, an 8km walk through ancient woodland passing many waterfalls and geological features. The nearby Three Peaks walk takes in Ingleborough, Pen-y-ghent and Whernside in its 40km ramble. Should that not be challenging enough there are also fell and cyclocross races. The routes described circumnavigate two of those three summits.

At the foot of Whernside, Ribblehead viaduct is a spectacular and alien presence among these bleak fells. Its 24 arches span 400m and reach 32m at their highest. It opened in 1874. The navvies and their families lived in a number of shanty towns for the four years of its construction.

In addition to accidents there were many deaths from smallpox and other infectious outbreaks. This lead to the extension of the graveyard at Chapel-le-Dale, where there is a commemorative plaque.

PARKING

There is a large car park and restricted short term on road parking in the centre of town. Further out there is unrestricted parking on residential streets.

ROUTE 8
Dentdale and round Whernside

Start/Finish	Main car park, Bank Top exit SD 693 730
Distance	44.9km/28.1 miles
Total climb	730m
Grade	Medium Challenging
Cycling time	2hr 20min
Café stops	Dent

Whernside is surrounded by four distinct Dales and each provides excellent, if sometimes challenging, cycling. Kingsdale is full of nothing but grand scenery, limestone scars, potholers and the occasional farm. Dentdale is lush, has hedges rather than walls and is named after the charming whitewashed village of Dent, complete with cobbled streets and all. Ribblesdale is exposed and often bleak with its famous viaduct. The dale of the River Doe has more limestone scars with good views of Ingleborough. The climbs out of Kingsdale and particularly Dentdale may seem long but where else would you rather do them?

Turn right, leaving the car park onto Bank Top, and immediately pass under the disused railway viaduct. Turn left and downhill to Thornton in Lonsdale and cross the two rivers. Pass the Waterfall Walk entrance and under the viaduct to leave town. Turn right (0.9km) to **Thornton in Lonsdale**. In Thornton in Lonsdale turn right (1.3km) opposite the Marton Arms Hotel to Dent. Climb steeply into **Kingsdale** and pass the turn (2.9km) with its panorama viewpoint. ◀

Continue the climb then descend into and along Kingsdale. Pass through the right hand gate (8.0km) at Kingsdale Head and resume the climb. Expect more gates. At 473m (11.0km) the watershed of **White Shaw Moss** is some 330m above Dent. Descend, **very steeply** at times, and be prepared to stop for closed gates. The

Views include not only Ingleborough to the east but the Lune Valley, Morecambe Bay and Lakeland Fells.

initial views are of Deepdale but gradually open out into Dentdale with the odd roadside waterfall to add interest. Turn left at the T-junction (15.9km) towards Dent and Sedbergh. Enter **Dent** and turn right at the monument to Adam Sedgewick (17.2km) towards Hawes.

Kingsdale

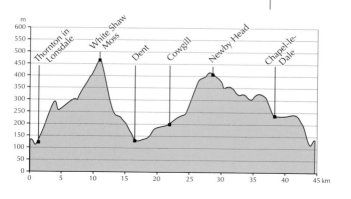

85

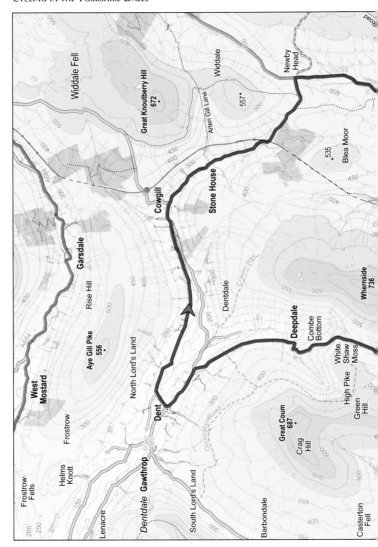

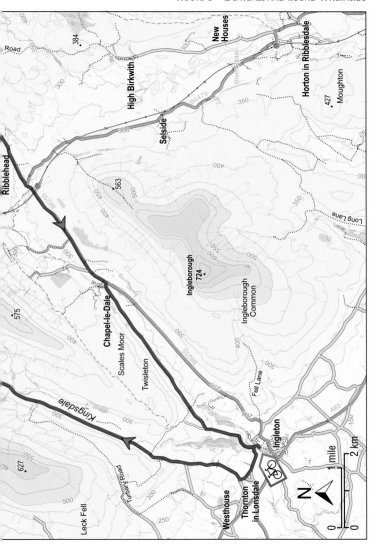

Dentdale is beautiful from top to bottom. The lower Dale is largely slate, whereas the upper Dale is limestone. This is reflected in the buildings and walls, where they exist, for Dentdale has many hedges. The popular village of Dent is very pretty with whitewashed cottages and cobbled streets. Late June sees a music and beer festival.

Dent railway station near Cowgill at 350m is the highest on the network in England.

Leave town, cross the River Dee and bend right towards Hawes and Dent station. The gently rolling ride up the valley is a joy. Pass the turn for Dent Station in **Cowgill** (23.3km) and continue towards Hawes and Newby Head. Cross the river and start the riverside climb out of the valley. The river is a pleasing companion. Pass the Sportsman Inn before recrossing the river and continue the climb passing under the viaduct. The road steepens then levels before reaching **Newby Head**. Turn

River Dee beyond Cowgill, Dentdale

right at the T-junction (28.9km) towards Ingleton. ▶ Views include Pen-y-ghent and the flat topped Ingleborough. Gradually the arches of the **Ribblehead Viaduct** come into view.

This rollercoaster of a road can be busy.

For more information on the **Ribblehead Viaduct** see the introduction to this chapter.

Pass the turn (34.8km) for Horton in Ribblesdale. Pass under the viaduct and enter the valley of the River Doe, following the course of a Roman road. Turn right (38.2km) to **Chapel-le-Dale** church. Pass the small church and graveyard. Continue on this narrow gated road, with Twisleton Scar above, back to Ingleton.

A walk over **Twisleton Scar**, with its limestone pavement, is a bit of a treat. Foreign boulders sit on the limestone. Some of these granite erratics were transported by glacier from Scotland.

To the left Ingleborough dominates the skyline, with the White Scar show caves at its foot. The final descent into town is twisty and through mature woodland. Turn left at the T-junction in **Ingleton**, cross the river and turn right towards Skipton. Turn right again at the top of the slope to return to the start.

ROUTE 9
Ribblesdale and round Ingleborough

Start/Finish	Main car park, Bank Top exit SD 693 730
Distance	37.9km/23.7 miles
Total climb	405m
Grade	Medium Moderate
Cycling time	1hr 50min
Café stops	Horton in Ribblesdale

Inspired by the Helwith Bridge Duathlon bike leg, this route circles Ingleborough. The route passes through limestone country. The only sharp climbs are out of Ingleton and Austwick. At the time of writing a bridleway is under construction alongside the A65.

Turn right leaving the car park onto Bank Top and immediately pass under the disused railway viaduct. Continue straight through the town centre. The road bends right and climbs. Turn left and uphill at the T-junction (0.5km) towards Hawes then turn right (0.8km) to Clapham. This is a wide road with views south to the Forest of Bowland.

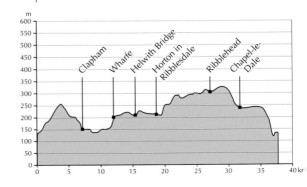

The climb is gradual before a steep descent into **Clapham**. Pass the turn signed Yorkshire Cycle Way (6.6km). Turn left at the T-junction (7.0km). Cross the beck then bend sharp right and left to get round the New Inn. At the A65 turn left (8.5km) towards Skipton either on the main road or the parallel bridleway. The road is usually very busy and carries a lot of freight. Turn left (8.9km) to Austwick.

In **Austwick**, at the green with the pillar (10.1km), turn left to Horton. The walled lane narrows and climbs through craggy and broken limestone country. Continue straight ahead at the crossroads (14.4km), with Pen-y-ghent dominating the skyline ahead. ▸ Descend into **Helwith Bridge**, where the duathlon route starts. Cross the river and railway line. Turn left at the T-junction (15.5km) to Horton in Ribblesdale. Enter and pass through **Horton in Ribblesdale** (18.4km). Bend left and cross the Ribble to leave Horton in the direction of Hawes.

> **Horton in Ribblesdale** is a pretty village with some interesting old buildings and a church that dates from the 12th century. Most visitors come for the walking and caving. Horton is a popular start and finish point for the Three Peaks Walk. The Pennine and Ribble Ways also pass through.

Ribblehead Viaduct with Whernside above

Watch out for quarry lorries.

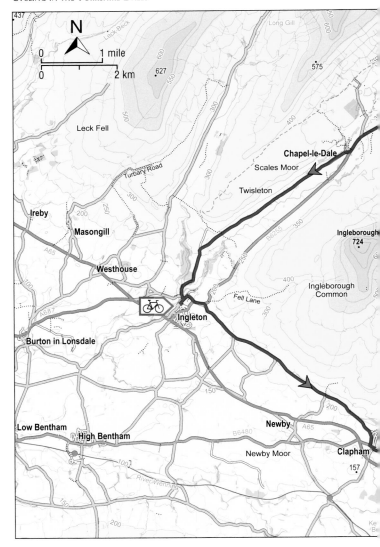

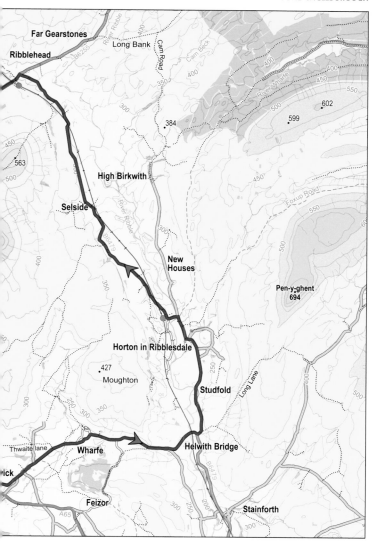

Bend right, parallel the railway and shortly pass under it. The undulating road gradually climbs with numerous sharp pulls and drops. Pass through **Selside**. The valley opens to reveal drumlins. As the northern extent of Ingleborough is passed the ridge of Whernside is revealed, along with the **Ribblehead Viaduct** at its foot.

For more information on the **Ribblehead Viaduct** see the introduction to this chapter.

Turn left at the T-junction (27.8km) towards Ingleton. Pass under the viaduct and enter the valley of the River Doe following the course of a Roman Road. Turn right (31.2km) to **Chapel-le-Dale** church. At this point the Helwith Bridge Duathlon route continues straight to Ingleton. Pass the church and graveyard. Continue on this narrow gated road with Twisleton Scar above all the way back to Ingleton.

A walk over **Twisleton Scar**, with its limestone pavement, is a bit of a treat. Foreign boulders sit on the limestone. Some of these granite erratics were transported by glacier from Scotland.

To the left Ingleborough dominates the skyline with the White Scar show caves at its foot. The final descent into town is twisty and through mature woodland. Turn left at the T-junction in **Ingleton**, cross the river and turn right towards Skipton. Turn right again at the top of the slope. Continue along this road to return to the start.

Ingleborough in the distance from Overclose (Route 11)

Settle's origins can be traced back to the 7th century. In 1249 it got its market charter: the market still continues on Tuesdays. Apart from farming, cotton spinning started in the late 18th century, harnessing the power of the River Ribble. The Settle–Carlisle railway opened in 1875. The Naked Man café dates back to 1663, making it one of the oldest in the country.

Malham is attractive in its own right but most visitors, including many students on field trips, come to see the geological features. Malham cove is an 80m sheer curved cliff. Malham beck emerges at the bottom while at the top a prime example of limestone pavement provides microclimates for lime loving plants. Peregrine falcons can be seen nesting near the top. Gordale Scar is a 100m deep ravine with a couple of waterfalls. Janet's Foss is a small and beautifully set waterfall. Malham Tarn is England's highest lake. The water is trapped by glacial deposits and its distinctly alkaline chemistry is very rare.

PARKING

There are several pay and display car parks close to the town centre.

ROUTE 10
Dales and Tarn

Start/Finish	Whitefriars Court car park SD 819 638
Distance	49.1km/30.7 miles
Total climb	855m
Grade	Long Challenging
Cycling time	3hr
Café stops	Malham (The Old Barn on the main road and Beck Hall signed off Cove Road)

A truly challenging ride. There are four significant climbs and they can be brutal. The valley sections provide contrasting interludes along the Ribble then later down Littondale. Allow plenty of time and get fuelled up.

Turn left, leaving the car park and immediately pass under the railway. Pass the turn for Langcliffe (0.3km) and continue straight ahead. Cross the Ribble, pass the swimming pool and turn right (0.6km) to Little Stainforth. Continue on this narrow road through **Stackhouse** and into **Little Stainforth**. Turn right (4.0km) into the unsigned

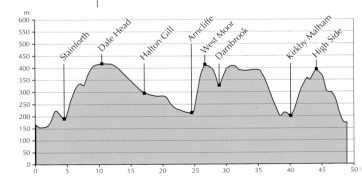

lane. Pass the campsite and continue down the very narrow lane. Ignore the dead end signs.

> The **packhorse bridge** dates back to the 1670s and just downstream is Stainforth Force, which is worth the short walk.

Cross the river, climb and turn right at the T-junction (4.6km) into **Stainforth**. Turn left (4.8km) and left again (4.9km) to Halton Gill. The climb is relentless and steep in places but there is generally little traffic. Pass the turn at Sannat Hall Farm (6.9km). Ahead lies Pen-y-ghent with its nose like southern ridge prominent on the left while to the right is Fountains Fell, the summit of which is hidden by its own slopes. Climb to **Dale Head** before a gentle descent along the flanks of Plover Hill. The gradient increases as Halton Gill and Littondale near. ▶ Cross the River Skirfare. Turn right (16.9km) immediately before **Halton Gill**, cross the small stream and continue down the valley to Litton and Arncliffe.

There are good long views down the valley.

Descent to Halton Gill, Littondale

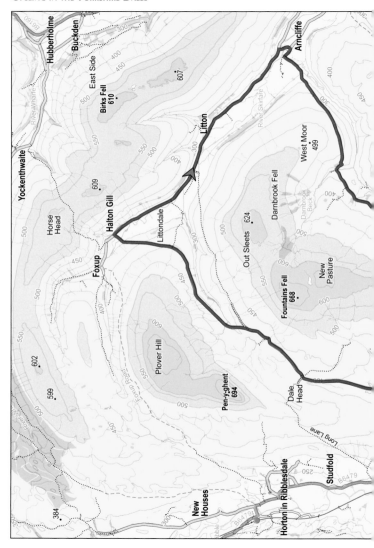

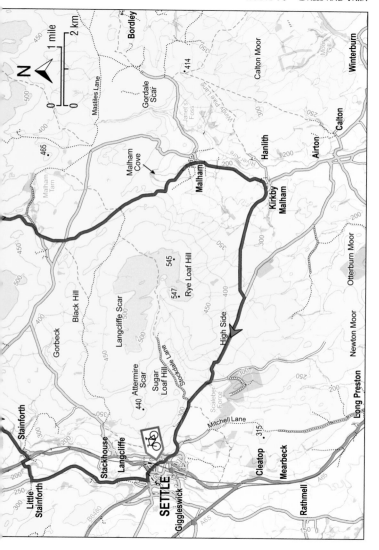

The floor of the dale is the only level cycling on this route. To the right you may either see the River Skirfare or just its bed depending on recent rainfall. This is one of those disappearing rivers. Pass through **Litton** (20.3km). Bend right (23.9km) into **Arncliffe**, cross the river and turn right (24.1km) into the small lane between two cottages leading to the village green. Turn right at the T-junction on the green by the village pump (24.2km) and head up the dale. Leave Arncliffe, cross Cowside Beck and bend left. The road parallels the beck before climbing steeply past Brootes Barn. Descend steeply into Darnbrook and climb again towards Malham Tarn. Pass the turn for the **Malham Tarn** Field Centre. Turn left (33.0km) to Malham, climb and continue straight ahead at the crossroads (33.7km) to Malham. The road remains level for a short distance with limestone pavement and bluffs all around. The descent starts gently but the gradient increases with a few sharp bends thrown in. Don't get too carried away or you may miss Malham Cove to the left. Enter **Malham** (38.1km) and continue straight ahead to Settle.

For more information on **Malham** see the introduction to this chapter.

In **Kirkby Malham** turn right where the main road bends left (40.2km) to Settle. Start the final climb of the route. Approaching **High Side** bend right by the turn for Airton. The route is now mostly downhill. Pass Scaleber Force. As Settle nears the rugged limestone of Attermire Scar can be seen to the north through to folds in the hills. The descent steepens.

Attermire Scar is one of several limestone exposures that mark the southern and western sides of Langcliffe Scar. The scars mark the line of the Craven Fault. At the western end Victoria Cave has yielded mammoth, bear, hippopotamus, rhinoceros and reindeer remnants plus man-made artefacts dating back to the last interglacial period.

Enter **Settle** (48.3km), continue straight ahead and downhill. Fork left (48.6km) over a short section of cobbles. Bend left in front of the large Elizabethan-style manor house. Turn right at the T-junction (48.8km) by the police station and continue through the town centre to return to the start.

Attermire and Langcliffe Scars

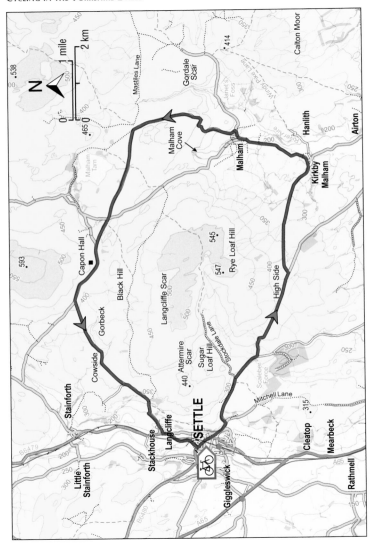

ROUTE 11

Langcliffe Scar and Malham

Start/Finish	Whitefriars Court car park SD 819 638
Distance	25.7km/16.1 miles
Total climb	545m
Grade	Short Challenging
Cycling time	1hr 25min
Café stops	Malham (The Old Barn on the main road and Beck Hall signed off Cove Road)

A short, steep, spectacular, cycling sojourn circumnavigating the scars of Langcliffe. With Malham in the middle this is a great ride in limestone country.

Turn right leaving the car park, then left (0.2km) diagonally across the square towards Airton. Turn left at the T-junction (0.4km), bend right then take the right fork in front of the large Elizabethan-style manor house towards Kirkby Malham and Airton. Pass over the cobbles and start the climb. Bend left (0.6km) uphill. Pass

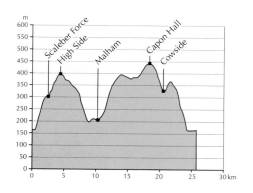

the junction (0.8km) and continue uphill. The climb is very steep in places and the lane narrows, but the climb does eventually ease (1.5km). To the left scars dominate the skyline.

> **Langcliffe Scar** consists of a series of limestone exposures which mark the line of the Craven Fault. At the western end Victoria Cave has yielded mammoth, bear, hippopotamus, rhinoceros and reindeer remnants plus man-made artefacts dating back to the last interglacial period.

Pass the stile (2.8km), unless a visit to **Scaleber Force** is called for. After a small dip the climb, steep in sections, resumes. Cross the cattle grid (4.4km) onto unenclosed grass covered moor. Bend left (5.5km) to Kirkby Malham by the turn for Airton. Cross the cattle grid (5.8km) into a walled lane and after a few undulations descend, sometimes steeply, into **Kirkby Malham**. Turn left at the T-junction (8.9km), in effect straight ahead, to Malham. Climb and descend into **Malham**.

Limestone landscape above Malham

For more information on **Malham** see the introduction to this chapter.

Turn right (10.8km) towards Gordale and Malham Tarn. Turn left (11.2km) towards Malham Tarn for a challenging climb out of the dale. On a sharp right bend (12.2km) a footpath leads to the top of Malham cove with its limestone pavement and giddy views.

The steep climb continues in a shallow dry valley but eventually eases (12.7km). Bend left (14.5km) towards Settle, gently descend and pass the outflow of **Malham Tarn**, where the climb resumes. Continue straight ahead at the crossroads (17.1km). Turn left at the T-junction (17.9km), in effect straight on, to Langcliffe and Settle. ▸

Bend left (19.6km) to Langcliffe and Settle. Descend to **Cowside** (21.1km) and climb round the back of the farm through beech trees. Cross the cattle grid into open grassland with views of Ingleborough, Pen-y-ghent and Ribblesdale. After a short climb the descent to Langcliffe begins in a shallow craggy valley. The descent has some tight corners and steep sections. Descend into **Langcliffe** and pass through with the church and green to the left. Turn left at the T-junction with the main road (24.3km) to Settle. Turn left at the T-junction (25.4km) and enter **Settle**. Pass under the viaduct to return to the start.

The route peaks at 446m (18.8km).

REETH

Approaching Aisgill with Wild Boar Fell in the distance (Route 13)

Few settlements have a location such as that enjoyed by Reeth, spread over a south facing slope and sheltered by hills to the north: sitting above the River Swale, and upstream from its confluence with Arkle Beck, Reeth's aspect is best revealed when approaching from the south.

Originally a Saxon settlement, Reeth was important enough to be included in the Domesday Book. Lead was mined before the Romans came and this continued until just over a century ago. The marks remain to be seen and visited in the surrounding hills. The town got its market charter in 1695.

PARKING

There is ample car parking on and around the town green, for which a donation is expected.

ROUTE 12

Tan Hill

Start/Finish	Town green SE 038 993
Distance	45.0km/28.1 miles
Total climb	580m
Grade	Medium Hard
Cycling time	2hr 15min
Café stops	Thwaite (Kearton Country Hotel), Muker and Gunnerside

The route is as natural as they come: head for Tan Hill up one dale, turn left and return by another. The outward route follows narrow and pretty Arkengarthdale for its entire length, before climbing across heather moorland to Tan Hill. At 528m (1732ft) the Tan Hill Inn is the highest pub in England. The return is along the prettiest dale of them all, Swaledale. Along the way the scars of almost two thousand years of lead mining mark the valleys and hillsides, nowhere more so than at Gunnerside Gill.

Take the road to Langthwaite leaving the green by the public conveniences. Climb round Reeth Low Moor, heading up Arkengarthdale, named after Arkle Beck.

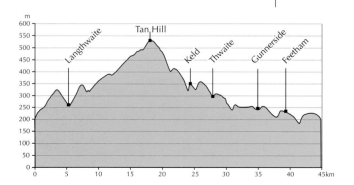

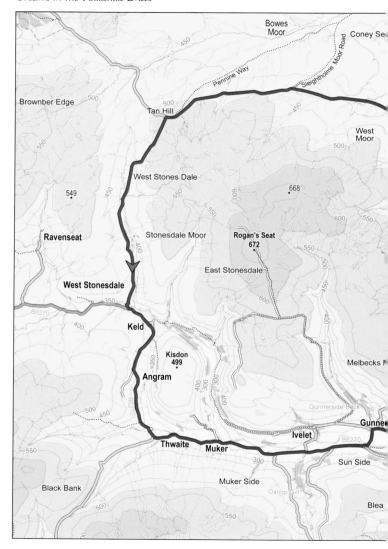

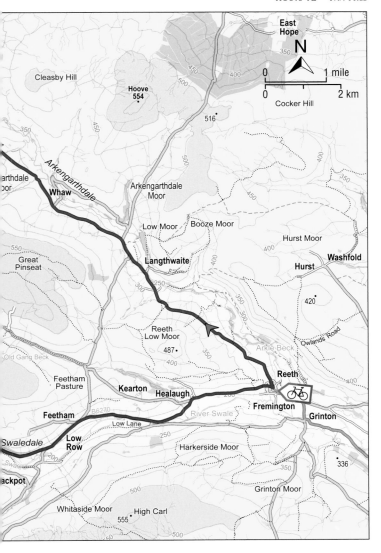

East
Hope

N

0   1 mile

0   2 km

Cocker Hill

Cleasby Hill

Hoove
554

516

arthdale
or

Arkengarthdale

Whaw

Arkengarthdale
Moor

Low Moor   Booze Moor

Hurst Moor

Langthwaite

Hurst

Washfold

Great
Pinseat

420

Old Gang Beck

Reeth
Low Moor

Arkle Beck

Owlands Road

487

Feetham
Pasture

Kearton   Healaugh

Reeth

Feetham

B6270

Low Lane

River Swale

Fremington

Grinton

Low
Row

Swaledale

Harkerside Moor

336

Swale

ackpot

Grinton Moor

Whitaside Moor   High Carl

555

*Approaching
Reeth, Swaledale*

Descend and pass through **Langthwaite** (5.0km), with its village square and pub, the Red Lion, just the other side of the small bridge. The route climbs, with some respite, to Tan Hill. Pass the CB (Charles Bathurst) Inn (5.8km) and pass the turn (6.1km) for Barnard Castle. The valley gradually broadens and heather moorland takes over. To the north the high Pennines come into view. Pass the blue 'W2W C2C' cycle route sign (14.8km). Continue to **Tan Hill**. The Tan Hill Inn is pretty obvious, unless the cloud is down, being the only building for miles.

Pass the inn and turn left (18.4km) to Keld and Thwaite. Descend with only one small climb and pass through **West Stonesdale**. Descend steeply and cross the River Swale. Turn left at the T-junction by the campsite (24.3km) to Keld and Reeth. Climb away from the river and pass through **Keld** (25.6km). Pass the 'Keld only' turns, unless a short walk to the waterfalls of Catrake and Kisdon Forces appeals, and it should. At this point the road and the River Swale separate only to rejoin beyond Muker. Climb and pass through **Angram**. Descend to and pass through **Thwaite** (28.3km). Pass the turn (28.6km) for Hawes.

◀ Pass through **Muker** (30.7km), with the Farmers Arms. Pass through **Gunnerside**, with the Kings Head (35.3km) on the corner, to Reeth and Richmond. Pass through **Low Row**, **Feetham** and **Healaugh**. As Reeth approaches the valley widens. Descend into **Reeth** to return to the start.

The return to Reeth is mostly down hill with only small climbs where the road moves away from the Swale to link villages and hamlets.

ROUTE 13

Wensleydale, Mallerstang and Tan Hill

Start/Finish	Town green SE 038 993
Distance	92.2km/57.6 miles: Birkdale and Swaledale option 87.2km/54.5 miles
Total climb	1250m: Birkdale and Swaledale option 1100m
Grade	Long Hard
Cycling time	5hr 10min: Birkdale and Swaledale option 4hr 50min
Café stops	Bolton Castle, Askrigg, Hardraw, Kirkby Stephen (The Pink Geranium and the Mulberry Bush): Birkdale and Swaledale option; Thwaite (Kearton Country Hotel), Muker and Gunnerside

So we come to the longest and hilliest ride, apart from Route 24. The route follows the River Ure as far as is possible on a cycle along Wensleydale and Mossdale, and then follows the River Eden through Mallerstang Common to Kirkby Stephen. The return via Tan Hill follows Arkle Beck. A significant portion of the route is outside the National Park, but few would notice or even care. There are two significant climbs: early on from Grinton into Wensleydale (463m), then much later from Barras to Tan Hill. At 528m (1732ft) the Tan Hill Inn is the highest pub in England.

From Nateby there is an alternative route back to Reeth which is fully described below. The option reduces both the distance and climb. It is a great ride in its own right. The climb from Nateby to Lamp Moss (518m) is not easy with some seriously steep section. From Nateby to Keld it can feel very bleak, with little in the way of human presence. The return to Reeth along Swaledale is, as always, a delight.

Leave Reeth by the through road at the lower end of the green towards Leyburn and Richmond. Cross Arkle Beck and pass through **Fremington**. Cross the River Swale and enter **Grinton**. Turn right (1.5km) where the road bends left at the Bridge Inn towards Leyburn and Redmire. The road is narrow and climbs steeply alongside the wooded Grinton Gill. Beyond the cattle grid the gradient eases and unenclosed moorland takes over. Turn right (2.2km)

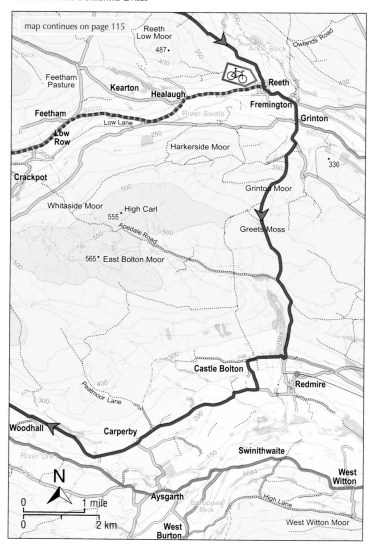

map continues on page 115

Reeth
Low Moor

487•

Feetham
Pasture

Kearton Healaugh

Feetham

Low Lane

Low
Row

Crackpot

Reeth

Fremington

Grinton

336•

Harkerside Moor

Grinton Moor

Whitaside Moor High Carl

555•

Apedale Road

Greets Moss

565• East Bolton Moor

Peatmoor Lane

Castle Bolton

Redmire

Woodhall

Carperby

River Ure

Swinithwaite

West
Witton

Aysgarth

High Lane

West Witton Moor

West
Burton

Bishopdale Beck

N

0   1 mile
0   2 km

Mossdale

towards Redmire. The climb is steep in sections with good view of Swaledale.

Pass over the cattle grid (5.3km) just before the summit of **Greets Moss** at 463m. Descend into Wensleydale. Pass the quarries on the left and keep alert for the next turn. Turn right (8.8km) to Castle Bolton. Pass through **Castle Bolton** and bend left, downhill, at the castle. Turn right at the T-junction (10.8km) to Carperby. Pass through **Carperby** and pass the turn for Aysgarth. Pass through **Woodhall** and Nappa. Continue on the road. Bend left, descend and pass the turn for Newbiggin (20.3km). Pass the turn for Muker and descend through **Askrigg**.

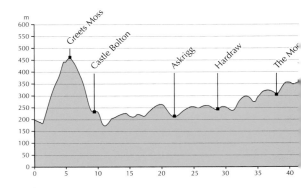

Dominated by the church of Saint Oswald, full of character and set in a sunny location, **Askrigg** has been a market town since 1587. Beside the market cross can be found a steel ring set into the pavement to which bulls were tethered in the days of baiting. There are a number of tea shops. The public toilets are in the village hall.

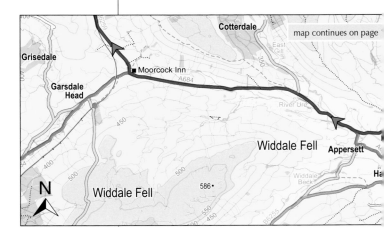

map continues on page

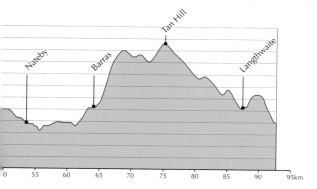

Continue along the dale on a road that never levels except for very short sections. Pass the turns for Bainbridge (22.8km), Hawes (28.4km) and Muker via Buttertubs Pass (28.9km). After a couple of short sharp climbs pass through **Hardraw** (29.7km).

At 30m **Hardraw Force** is the largest single drop waterfall in England. Access is via the Green Dragon Inn.

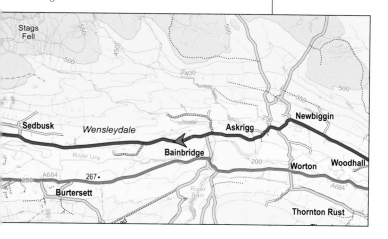

115

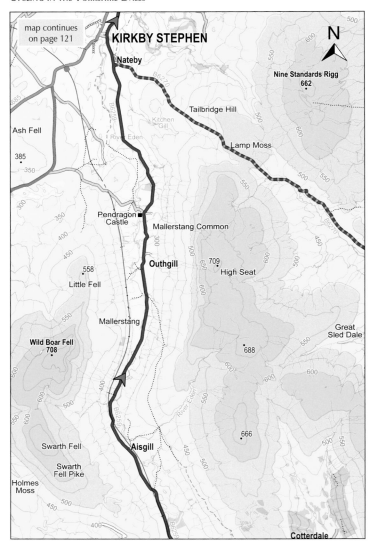

map continues
on page 121

KIRKBY STEPHEN

Nateby

Tailbridge Hill

Lamp Moss

Nine Standards Rigg
662

Ash Fell

385

River Eden

Kitchen Gill

Pendragon Castle

Mallerstang Common

Outhgill

High Seat
709

558
Little Fell

Mallerstang

Great Sled Dale

Wild Boar Fell
708

688

Swarth Fell

Aisgill

River Eden

666

Swarth Fell Pike

Holmes Moss

Cotterdale

Turn right at the T-junction (30.8km) towards Kirkby Stephen and Sedbergh. The road parallels the River Ure for a short distance before repeatedly climbing then descending. Pass the turn for Cotterdale (32.7km), which is a dead end. Turn right at the **Moorcock Inn** (37.2km) to Kirkby Stephen. ▶ At **Aisgill** the route enters Cumbria alongside the River Eden.

Mallerstang Common and the River Eden

Descend Mallerstang Common. The hillsides rise steeply particularly to the east with Mallerstang Edge clearly defined. Pass through **Outhgill** (47.2km), watching out for red squirrels. Pass the turn (48.4km) at Pendragon Castle.

The road parallels and criss-crosses the Settle–Carlisle Railway.

Legend has it that **Pendragon Castle** was built by King Arthur's father Uther Pendragon. It is actually 12th century.

The valley widens and flattens for a short riverside stretch before resuming the undulations. Pass through **Nateby**, where the Birkdale option starts (52.9km).

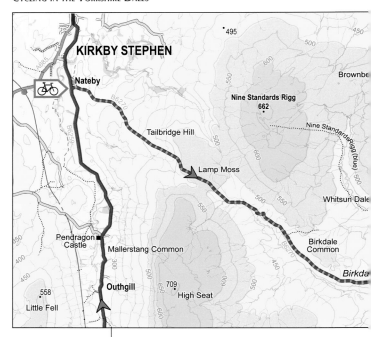

Birkdale and Swaledale option

Turn right (52.9km) in Nateby to Swaledale and Reeth.
A very short descent is followed by a steep climb. The
climb continues with respite rather than rest. Much of
the early climb is in a small valley. As height is gained
Mallerstang Common comes into view. Once the
small valley is left the climb continues on the flank of
Tailbridge Hill with the final challenging section visible
ahead. Gird those loins and get on with it. At the top the
road levels. Re-enter Yorkshire at **Lamp Moss** (57.9km).
There is little evidence of human habitation since
Nateby and things aren't about to change soon. The
grasslands have been replaced by dun coloured heather
hills. The rocks are darker, black in places. The skyline is
ringed by high hills with Great Shunner Fell dominant.

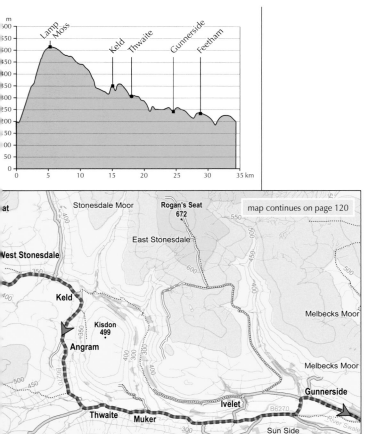

The route continues on a sinuous rollercoaster of a road that follows the shape of the dale side as it descends. Pass the turn for Ravenseat (63.2km).

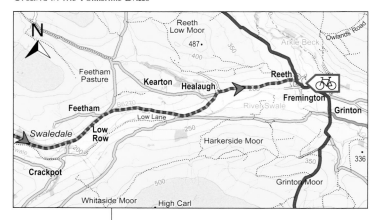

With the gradient easing cross the Swale at Hoggarths and enter Swaledale. Pass the turn by the camp site for Tan Hill (66.7km) and continue to Keld and Reeth.

Climb from the river and pass through **Keld** (68.0km). Pass the 'Keld only' signs, unless a short walk to the waterfalls of Catrake and Kisdon Forces appeals, and

*Hoggarths, upper
Swaledale*

it should. At this point the road and the River Swale separate, only to rejoin beyond Muker. Climb and pass through **Angram**. Descend and pass through **Thwaite** (70.7km). Pass the turn (71.0km) for Hawes.

The return to Reeth is mostly downhill, with only small climbs where the road moves away from the Swale to link villages and hamlets. Pass through **Muker** (73.1km), with the Farmers Arms. Pass through **Gunnerside** with the Kings Head (77.7km) on the corner to Reeth and Richmond. Pass through **Low Row**, **Feetham** and **Healaugh**. As Reeth approaches the valley widens. Descend into **Reeth** to return to the start.

Main route via Kirkby Stephen
Cross the River Eden and enter the outskirts of **Kirkby Stephen** (53.8km). Continue straight ahead, bend left then turn right at the traffic lights to the town centre (55.1km).

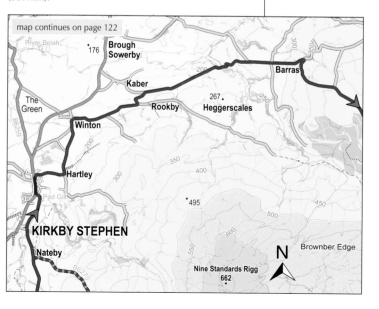

map continues on page 122

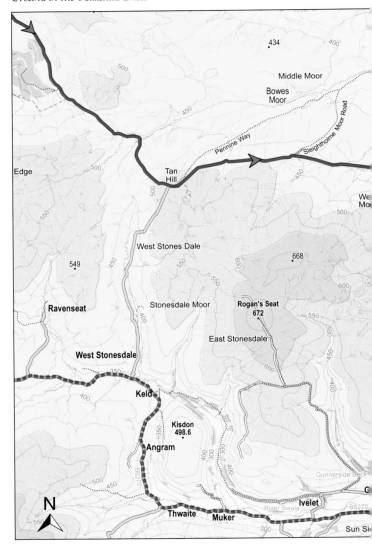

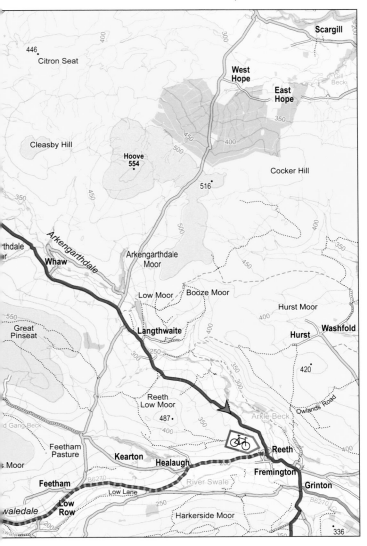

Kirkby Stephen is a busy market town and has been since 1361. The red sandstone buildings are host to many tea shops and cafés, so stock up here as there are not many more opportunities on the remainder of the route.

Head north and continue straight ahead at the small roundabout (55.3km). Turn right (55.4km) almost immediately to **Hartley**. Cross the Eden. Turn left at the T-junction in Hartley (56.4km) to Winton. In **Winton** turn right at the crossroads on the village green (57.9km), signed 'unsuitable for heavy goods vehicles'. Continue straight ahead (58.9km). Turn left at the T-junction (59.8km) in the hamlet of **Rookby** by Low House and not towards Heggerscales. Turn right at the T-junction (60.3km) onto a wide road. ◄

The North Pennines dominate to the left.

Ahead and slightly to the right, above the conifer plantation near the skyline, is the top of the last big climb of the day. Cross the river (62.5km) and climb steeply. Pass the turn (63.5km) for Brough then straight ahead at the crossroads (64.1km) by the Mouthlock Centre and climb through **Barras**. Turn right (65.1km) after a steep climb, and immediately after the disused railway, to **Tan Hill**. The climb is steep but the views are a good distraction. Pass the unsigned turn (66.6km). The elevation is over 450m and remains so for some distance. This section is a joy after the climb as the road swoops, dips and climbs on this high plateau before re-entering Yorkshire at the cattle grid. Pass the turn (72.7km) for Keld then pass the Tan Hill Inn towards Reeth and Barnard Castle.

Pass the turn (76.3km) with blue cycleway signs for 'W2W C2C'. The route is along Arkengarthdale all the way to Reeth. The heather moorland gradually changes to grass pasture and the dale narrows. Pass the turn (85.0km) for Barnard Castle and pass the CB Inn. Pass through **Langthwaite** (86.1km) with its village square and pub, the Red Lion, just the other side of the small bridge. Crest one last significant climb over **Reeth Low Moor** and descend into **Reeth**.

ROUTE 14
Richmond

Start/Finish	Town green SE 038 993
Distance	52.4m/32.8 miles: Marske option 35.7km/22.3 miles
Total climb	730m: Marske option 535m
Grade	Long Hard: Marske option Medium Hard
Cycling time	2hr 55min: Marske option 1hr 55min
Café stops	Main route: Richmond (several) and Fremington (The Dales Bike Centre); Marske option Fremington (The Dales Bike Centre)

A route that contrasts with and complements the others from Reeth. Plenty of undulating roads, high moors and a visit to Richmond. Most of the roads are virtually traffic free, for reasons which will become obvious. There is a short track section which many would consider to be unrideable but this can be avoided using the Marske Option for the return from Richmond.

The main valley road offers the cyclist an acceptable route back to Reeth. However, the Marske option offers quieter roads, better views and a bit more exploration at the cost of more effort.

Leave Reeth by the road at the lower end of the green towards Leyburn and Richmond. Cross Arkle Beck and pass through **Fremington**. Cross the Swale, enter **Grinton** and bend left at the Bridge Inn (1.5km) towards Richmond. Turn right (6.6km) towards Stainton and Leyburn. Pass the turn (8.4km) for **Stainton**. Turn right at the T-junction (9.9km) towards Leyburn and Bellerby. Turn left at the T-junction (11.2km) towards Catterick Garrison. Turn left at the right bend (11.5km) onto an unsigned road and pass a couple of concrete bunkers. This section across a military training area of grass moors and occasional plantations peaks at 299m (14.0km).

Pass through **Brokes** (17.1km). Descend into a small step sided valley (18.5km), climb and pass the turn for Hudswell (18.9km). Pass through Holly Hill, descend,

Market Place, Richmond

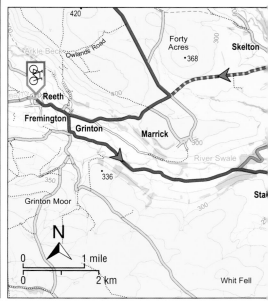

cross the Swale and enter **Richmond** (19.6km). Pass the first right turn then fork right at the left bend by the house with the sundial. Climb, bend right at the cobbled road and continue into the market square (20.0km).

> Founded in 1071 by the Normans, **Richmond** has been recognised by many visitors as a romantic treasure. The castle, on a spur overlooking the river, was completed in 1086. The town's predominant Georgian architecture was financed largely by the boom in lead mining and the wool trade during the 17th and 18th centuries. Trinity Church, in the

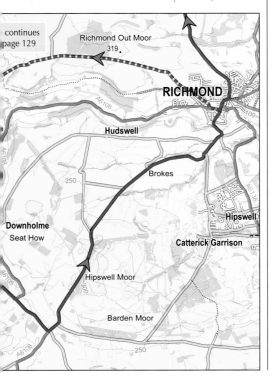

continues
page 129

enormous cobbled market place, houses Green Howards Regimental Museum. Sadly use of the market place as a car park does reduce its charm considerably. The Georgian Theatre Royal, founded in 1788, has been fully refurbished.

Swaledale from the descent into Fremington

Marske option
Leave Richmond's market square by the Kings Head Hotel, turn left at the roundabout towards Leyburn and

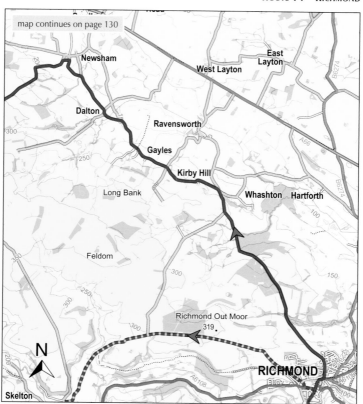

map continues on page 130

Newsham

West Layton

East Layton

Dalton

Ravensworth

Gayles

Kirby Hill

Long Bank

Whashton   Hartforth

Feldom

Richmond Out Moor
319

N

RICHMOND

Skelton

Reeth. Turn right at the petrol station (20.4km) and climb gently beside the cricket ground. Bend left: the climb increases leaving Richmond. The road peaks beside two transmitter towers at 313m (24.0km) on **Richmond Out Moor**. Pass the turn for Whashton and descend, steeply at times, to **Marske**. Bend left in Marske and turn right at the T-junction (28.3km) towards Marrick, Reeth and Hurst. Climb, steeply at first, descend, cross a steam then climb to the crossroads. Continue straight ahead at the

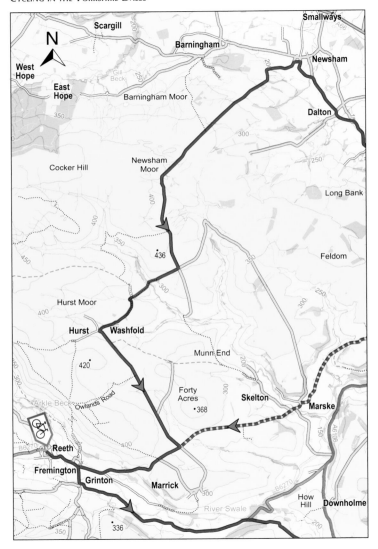

crossroads (31.7km) to Reeth with one last climb. Pass the turn (32.3km) for Marrick and descend, steeply at times. Turn right at the T-junction in **Fremington** (34.7km) to **Reeth** to return to the green.

Main route

Leave the square by the Kings Head Hotel, continue straight ahead at the two roundabouts, climb and bend right. Turn left at the traffic lights (20.6km) towards Ravensworth and climb steeply for the next kilometre. Pass the turn (26.3km) for Marske. Turn left (27.0km) at the staggered crossroads to Kirby Hill. Pass through **Kirby Hill** (27.8km) complete with church and pub. Descend and pass through the strung out village of **Gayles** (29.8km). Bend left (30.6km). In **Dalton** turn right at the T-junction (31.2km) and then almost immediately turn left (31.3km) to Newsham. In **Newsham** turn left (33.1km) before the yellow salt box and left again at the T-junction (33.3km). The walled lane climbs through pasture with good views all around. ▶ The road peaks at just over 400m (38.4km) and then passes through two gates onto open moorland. Enjoy the ride on the ribbon of road laid out ahead.

Beware the false summits.

Cattle grid high on the moor road

Descend to the crossroads (41.1km). The road ahead stops at Helwith but mountain bikers could continue on the bridleways to Marske. The left turn is often closed due to military exercises on the army ranges. Hence so little traffic. So turn right and ignore the dead end sign. Descend and continue straight ahead where the asphalt ends (41.8km). Do not bend left to the farmhouse. This is the off-road section. Push or port your cycle. Cross the stream by the bridge and climb out. As the gradient eases the rideability of the grass track improves. Pass through a number of gates. Continue straight ahead (42.9km) where a track joins from the right. The road surface gradually improves. Turn left and uphill at the T-junction in **Walshfold** (44.3km). Climb, descend, climb and descend. Turn right at the crossroads (48.3km) to Reeth for one last climb. Pass the turn (48.9km) for Marrick and descend, steeply at times. Turn right at the T-junction in **Fremington** (51.4km) to **Reeth** and return to the start.

SEDBERGH

Approaching Rawthey Bridge, Cautley Crag in the background (Route 16)

Sedbergh is the most westerly market town in the National Park. It sits tucked at the foot of the Howgill Fells, with the River Rawthey to the south. The Howgill Fells are composed largely of slate and this dark grey rock gives the local buildings their character. Many buildings in the area and into Dentdale have been whitewashed. Sedbergh's economy was based on the wool industry but this has gone and the town now depends on agriculture, tourism, light industry and the independent schools. Recently there has been a move to develop the town as a 'book town', the northern Hay-on-Wye.

PARKING

There are two car parks close to the centre of Sedbergh, with more on street options further out. The Joss Lane car park is used for the weekly Wednesday market.

ROUTE 15
Lune Valley and Barbondale

Start/Finish	A684, outside Duo Café, where Main Street becomes one way SD 657 921
Distance	44.1km/27.6 miles
Total climb	485m
Grade	Medium Moderate
Cycling time	2hr 10min
Café stops	Kirkby Lonsdale and Dent

For those not in the know the Lune Valley is something of a cycling treat. Between Sedbergh and Kirkby Lonsdale there are peaceful, hedged lanes and no real settlements. Beautiful and relaxing rather than spectacular. From Kirkby the stakes are raised. After a few small villages the route climbs away from the river and enters Barbondale with its long steady climb through the wilds. A sharp descent ends in Dent, the capital of the ever charming Dentdale. A short and pleasant ride leads back to Sedbergh.

Leave Sedbergh heading west on Main Street – away from the one-way section. Pass the Post Office, heading towards Kendal and the M6. Turn left (1.1km) towards Kirkby Lonsdale and Lancaster. Turn sharp right at Four Lane Ends (4.0km) towards the M6, where the main road bends left. Cross the **River Lune** and immediately turn left (4.7km) towards Killington and Old Hutton. ◄ Continue straight ahead at the crossroads (6.5km) towards Kirkby Lonsdale and Old Town. The road turns away from the valley bottom (9km) and climbs quite steeply. Turn left at the unsigned crossroads (9.8km) heading due south. Continue through pleasant undulating pasture with views across the valley to the Middleton and Barbon fells. The road is sometimes in park-like shallow valleys, sometimes on the valley side and occasionally through patches of woodland. Enter **Keartswick** and turn left at

The narrow hedged lane starts off alongside the river which is rather idyllic.

134

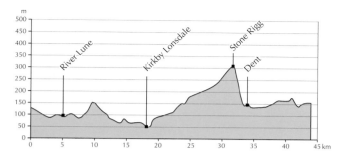

the T-junction (16.6km) to Kirkby Lonsdale. Continue into and pass through **Kirkby Lonsdale**. Keep to the main road and pass the market square to the left.

> **Kirkby Lonsdale** developed as a crossing point of the River Lune for packhorses and drove roads and got its market charter in 1227.

Turn left at the T-junction with the A65 (18.5km) towards Skipton and Ingleton. Immediately turn left

Barbondale

135

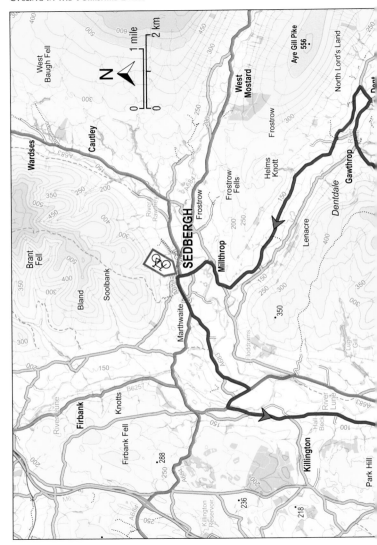

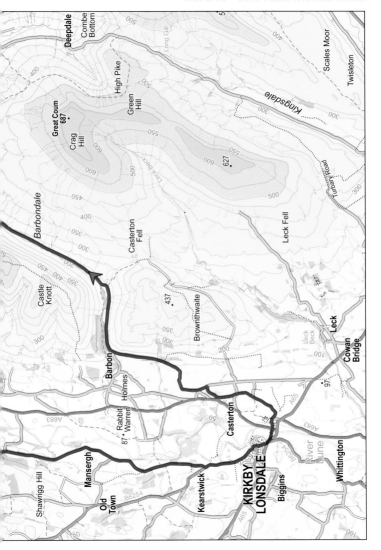

137

(18.6km) into a dead end section of road used for parking. Beware of the pedestrians, bikers and cyclists who congregate here. Cross the river and continue straight ahead at the cross road (18.9km) into a one-way lane used for parking. Continue straight ahead (19.0km) where the road bends right. Climb steeply up the very narrow lane tucked away in the corner by a litter bin. There are a number of narrow hedged lanes with grass growing down the middle for some time to come. Pass the caravan site and turn left at the T-junction (19.3km), which is in effect straight ahead. Bend left (19.4km) rather than go to Chapel House. Pass through High **Casterton** (20.2km). Continue straight ahead at the crossroads (20.7km) to Low Casterton.

Turn right at the T-junction in front of the church (21.2km). Climb through the village. Pass under the disused railway. Turn left at T-junction (21.7km) towards Barbon. Turn right (22.0km) to Dent and Sedbergh, rather than re-crossing the disused railway. Bend right and climb gently. ◄ Pass through the woods of Whelprigg and emerge onto a bracken covered hillside, with Barbondale ahead and views across the Lune to the left. Turn right at the T-junction (25.0km) to Dent and Sedbergh and enter **Barbondale**. After an initial climb descend closer to the semi-wooded Barbon Beck, which becomes treeless Barkin Beck where the climb restarts. The road is narrow, the climb far from challenging and the riding rather good. The climb ends beside **Stone Rigg** at 307m (31.7km) with Dentdale ahead. The descent is far steeper than the ascent – so take care. In **Gawthrop** turn right at the T-junction (33.0km) to Dent. Descend and turn right at the T-junction (33.4km), again to Dent. Enter and pass through **Dent**. Keep left at the George and Dragon towards Hawes.

The farm buildings start to take on a more rugged demeanour.

Dentdale is beautiful from top to bottom. The lower Dale is largely slate, whereas the upper Dale is limestone. This is reflected in the buildings and walls, where they exist, for Dentdale has many hedges. The popular village of Dent is very pretty

with whitewashed cottages and cobbled streets. Late June sees a music and beer festival.

Dent railway station near Cowgill at 350m is the highest on the network in England.

Whitewashed buildings in Dent, Dentdale

Cross the River Dee and immediately turn left (35.0km) into narrow lane unsigned apart from flood warnings. Another narrow lane with grass down the middle. Turn right at the T-junction (36.7km), in effect straight ahead, with the main road. Continue on this road back to Sedbergh. The road down the dale undulates past picturesque farm buildings, historic manor houses and patches of woodland with the River Dee in the bottom. Pass through **Millthrop**, cross the River Rawthey and climb back into **Sedbergh**. Continue straight ahead to return to the start.

ROUTE 16

Circuit of the Howgill Fells

Start/Finish	On A684, outside the Duo Café, where Main Street becomes one way SD 657 921
Distance	45.1km/28.2 miles: with Mallerstang extension 62.9km/39.3 miles
Total climb	490m; with Mallerstang extension 625m
Grade	Medium Moderate: with Mallerstang extension Long Moderate
Cycling time	2hr 15min: with Mallerstang extension 3hr
Café stops	Tebay (The Old School Tea Room)

Rising to 676m, the Howgill Fells are too often overlooked in favour of the Lake District to one side and the Dales to the other. Grass-covered and unenclosed, they provide excellent walking. Apart from Cautley Crag, rocky outcrops are few. You are likely to come across the wild horses that graze the fells. The circuit of the Howgills is a very natural route. The roads are quiet and the scenery surprisingly varied.

There is an option to extend the route up Garsdale and down Mallerstang Common before rejoining the main route at Ravenstonedale. The extension adds 17.8km and 136m to the main route. It is described from the start as far as Ravenstonedale where it rejoins the main route. Both Garsdale and Mallerstang Common provide good riding in a spectacular if sometimes bleaker landscape.

Leave Sedbergh heading east on Main Street, in compliance with the one way system. Turn left at the T-junction (0.3km) towards Kirkby Stephen and Hawes. Pass the turn (0.5km) towards Hawes, where the Mallerstang extension starts.

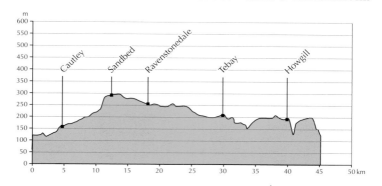

Garsdale and Mallerstang Common extension

Turn right off the main route towards Hawes. The route climbs up Garsdale, often alongside the River Clough with its many small waterfalls. The Dale is narrow and high sided with farms full of local character and little else. Pass through **Garsdale** (9.2km). The road peaks at the scattered community of **Garsdale Head** (14.5km). Pass under the railway viaduct and descend into Yorkshire. Turn left at the **Moorcock Inn** (15.8km) to Kirkby Stephen. ▶

The road parallels and criss-crosses the Settle-Carlisle Railway.

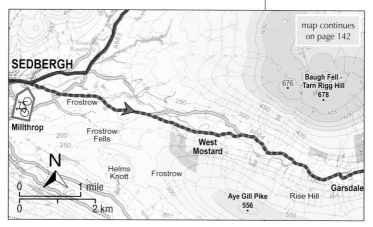

map continues on page 142

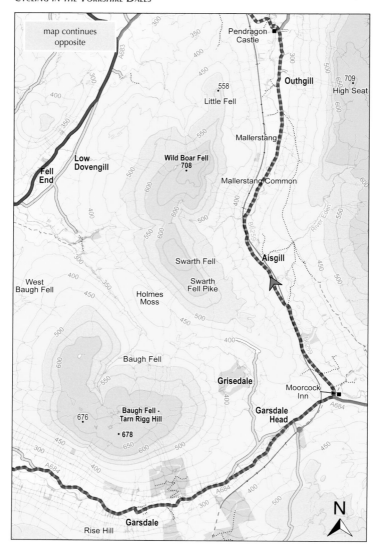

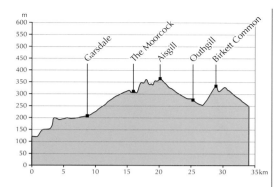

At **Aisgill** the route passes into Cumbria alongside the River Eden. Descend Mallerstang Common. Here the hills rise steeply, particularly to the east, with Mallerstang Edge clearly defined. Pass through **Outhgill** (25.8km), with its red squirrels. Turn left at **Pendragon Castle** (27.0km) onto an unsigned road.

> Legend has it that **Pendragon Castle** was built by King Arthur's father Uther Pendragon. It is actually 12th century.

Cross the River Eden and climb, via a series of bends, the unenclosed **Birkett Common**. Descend and turn left at the T-junction (30.0km). Turn right (31.2km) onto a

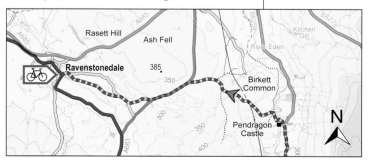

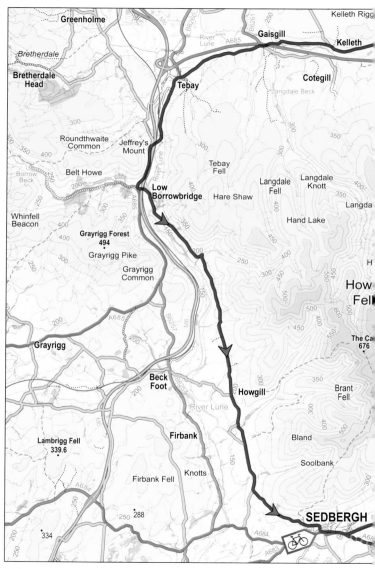

144

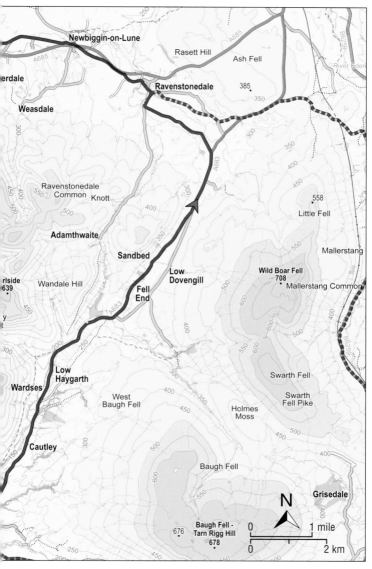

narrow unenclosed road. Pass the turn for the campsite (31.9km), cross the cattle grid into a walled lane then keep left at the fork (32.2km). Pass a right turn (33.6km), bend left and enter **Ravenstonedale**. Turn right at the T-junction (33.9km) to rejoin the main route outside the Black Swan Hotel at 17.4km.

Main route
After the Hawes turnoff, the road climbs alongside the River Rawthey, with the steep flanks of the Howgills to the left. There are a few descents where the road closes in on the river. Pass through **Cautley**.

> **Cautley Crag** and **Cautley Spout** (England's highest waterfall) reveal themselves in a deep dale on the right. A walk to them is always worth the effort.

Pass **Sandbed** and the nature of the country changes: limestone replaces slate, the countryside flattens considerably and the ridges emanating from The Calf diminish. The roads roll rather than climb. Turn left by the Fat Lamb public house (14.6km) to Ravenstonedale. Enter **Ravenstonedale** and pass the turn for Artlegarth.

After Sandbed limestone country returns

> **Ravenstonedale** is a pretty village on the watershed
> between the Lune and the Eden. It has a colony of
> timid red squirrels.

Pass the village green on the left. Bend left at the Black
Swan Hotel (17.4km) towards Kendal. The junction on the
bend marks the end of the Mallerstang option. Pass the
Old Vicarage and fork left. Turn left at the T-junction by
the Kings Head. Pass the Greenside turn. Take the cycle
path on the left, bend left and parallel the A685. Turn left
at the end of the cycle path (19.1km) and pass through
Newbiggin-on-Lune. At the main road turn left at the
T-junction (20.1km) towards Kendal, and immediately turn
right then left to Kelleth. This quiet, wide road traverses
along the side of the valley and has good views over
the Howgills. Pass through **Kelleth** and pass the turn for
Raisbeck and Orton. Descend to the main road and turn
right at the T-junction (26.5km) and almost immediately
turn left into **Gaisgill**. Pass through Gaisgill, followed by
a gentle climb to **Tebay**. In Tebay turn left at the T-junction
(29.1km) towards Grayrigg by the Old School Tea Room.

> **Tebay** largely owes its existence to the railways.
> Before that it was a staging post on the turnpike and
> the Romans have also been. It marks a considerable
> narrowing of the Lune valley and another notice-
> able change in the nature of the countryside.

Descend through Tebay and cross the West Coast
Rail Line and M6 motorway. Descend and turn left
(32.6km) to Carlingill. Pass under the railway and motorway. Turn left in **Low Borrowbridge** (33.1km), signed
'Unsuitable for Heavy Vehicles'. The road is narrow and
follows the line of the hillsides in almost straight lines
with some sharp dips and climbs to cross the numerous
becks and gills as a result. This is what the Romans did for
us. The road remains narrow irrespective of whether it is
walled, hedged or open. Beware, some of the dips tend
to collect grit. At **Howgill** continue straight ahead at the
crossroads (39.4km). Bend left (42.2km) to Sedbergh for

*The Lune Valley near
Low Borrowbridge*

the final climb of the day before a sweeping descent into **Sedbergh**. Stop for an ice cream at Lockbank Farm should the fancy take you. Pass the playing fields. Turn left at the T-junction with Main Street and in a few metres return to the start.

ROUTE 17
Barbondale and Holme Open Farm

Start/Finish	On A684, outside the Duo Café, where Main Street becomes one way SD 657 921
Distance	29.7km/18.6 miles
Total climb	385m
Grade	Short Hard
Cycling time	1hr 30min
Café stops	Holme Open Farm

For the non-cyclist there is little reason to visit Barbondale. No shops, no pubs, no picturesque villages; just big hills, a deep valley and a babbling stream. Even Barbon village is in the Lune Valley. This route sandwiches Barbondale between the delights of Dentdale and the Lune Valley.

Leave Sedbergh heading south on Finkle Street in the direction of Dent. Continue straight ahead at the roundabout towards Dent. Pass the turn for Kendal. Continue downhill, cross the river, bend right and climb gently. Pass the turn for Sedbergh golf club (1.8km). After a short descent turn right (3.1km) towards Holme Open Farm. Cross the **River Dee** at Rash Bridge, turn left and climb through the trees. The road on this side of the valley is the thread that links the settlements; some of which are more wary of the river than others. Expect serene riverside and sharp climbs in equal measure.

After an extended climb enter **Gawthrop** and turn right (7.8km) towards Barbon and Kirkby Lonsdale. There is 130m of climb spread over 1.5km to the top. The climb can be quite challenging in sections but soon ends at **Stone Rigg** and Barbondale is revealed. The 5km of descent is a joy. When the dale bends there is a gentle climb away from the river beside a rare conifer plantation.

Pass the turn (15.8km) and continue to Barbon. Descend into **Barbon**, pass the church and turn right

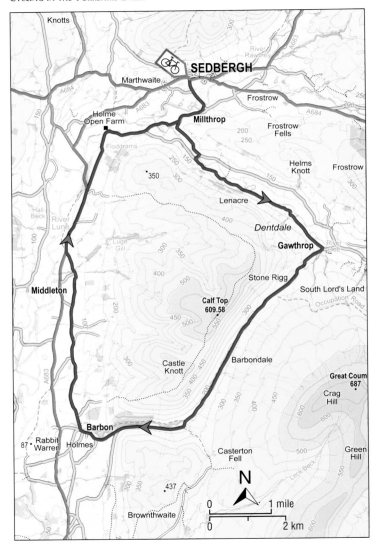

opposite the Wesleyan Chapel (17.1km). Continue north on this narrow hedged lane. Pass through **Middleton**. Continue straight ahead at High Green (21.6km) and cross the larger stream by a stone bridge. Turn left then right at two adjacent T-junctions (22.2km) by the entrance to Middleton Hall to join the main road heading north.

Turn right (24.0km) where the road bears left to Holme Open Farm. The road is straight but narrow and hilly. Pass the entrance to **Holme Open Farm** (25.7km). ▶ Climb steeply and cross the disused railway.

Dentdale

There is a café and camping here.

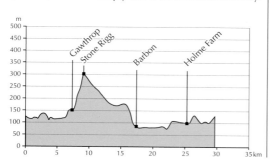

151

Pass through the gate (26.1km) and climb through open pasture. Fork left (26.8km) onto the road with a sign for a narrow bridge. Descend to the narrow bridge, passing through a gate on the way. Cross the river, follow the road through the golf course and climb to the main road. Turn left at the T-junction with the main road (27.9km). Pass through **Millthrop**, cross the River Rawthey and climb back into **Sedbergh**. Continue straight ahead to return to the start.

HAWES

Meadows approaching Hubberholme, Wharfedale (Route 20)

The main town of upper Wensleydale, Hawes has held a regular market since it got its charter in 1699. This is currently held every Tuesday. Its name derives from Old Norse and means 'pass between the mountains'. Hawes is a popular spot for visitors and is nearly always busy. There are several museums and the Wensleydale Creamery has a visitor centre.

Askrigg, dominated by the church of Saint Oswald, is full of character, is set in a sunny location and has been a market town since 1587. Beside the market cross can be found a steel ring set into the pavement to which bulls were tethered in the days of baiting. There are a number of tea shops. The public toilets are in the village hall.

PARKING

There are several pay and display car parks in Hawes and very limited on street parking.

ROUTE 18
The Big Cheese

Start/Finish	National Park Visitor Centre car park east of the town centre SD 875 898
Distance	62.5km/39.1 miles
Total climb	1220m
Grade	Long Challenging
Cycling time	3hr 30min
Café stops	Muker, Thwaite (Kearton Country Hotel) and Hardraw

This is challenging route: Wensleydale, Swaledale, Dentdale and Widdale linked by the climbs of Oxnop, Buttertubs, Galloway Gate & Coal Road and Newby Head. It is based on the cycle leg of the Wensleydale Triathlon, which actually starts in Semerwater and joins this route near Askrigg. The route can easily be done as two rides, as described in the text. Whether done for the challenge or competition (2hr 12min 2sec was the fastest time in 2012) it is undoubtedly a great ride that will be appreciated in hindsight.

Turn right leaving the car park and immediately turn right again towards Hardraw and Muker. Cross the wide valley floor and cross the River Ure. After a short climb turn right (1.4km) towards **Sedbusk** and Askrigg. The undulating road heads down the dale on a shelf raised well above the river. Pass side turns and enjoy the ride. Enter **Askrigg** and climb the Main Street.

> For more information on **Askrigg** see the introduction to this chapter.

At the top of Main Street turn left (9.3km) to Muker. Over the next three kilometres the road climbs 250m over Askrigg and **Oxnop Commons**. This may not appear overly challenging at first but

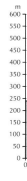

the gradient steepens and eases several times, making for some tough going. The top is reached at 498m (12.3km). Start the descent into Swaledale then fork left (12.7km). The narrowness of Swaledale becomes clear as progress is made. The road is narrow and steepens considerably with sharp bends towards the bottom. Take care.

Approaching Muker from Oxnop, Swaledale

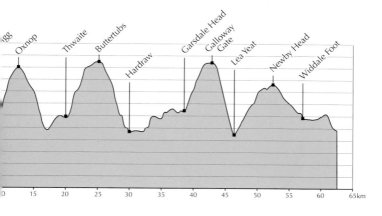

155

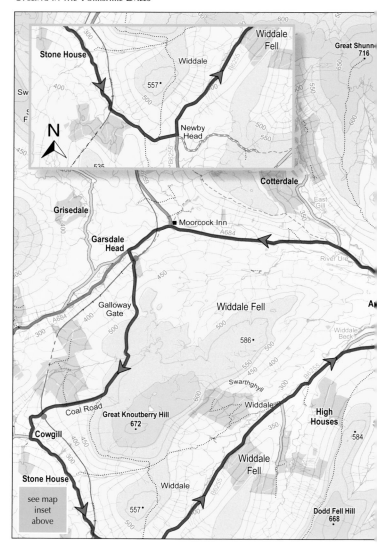

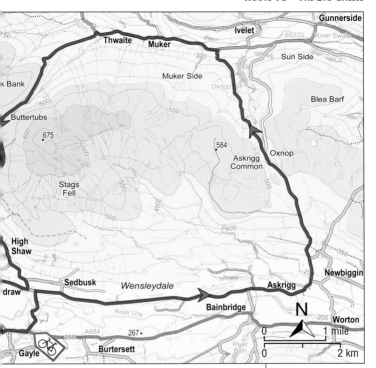

Turn left at the T-junction in the valley bottom (16.5km) to **Muker**. Pass through Muker and pass Usha Gap campsite where the climb restarts. Pass the turn for Hawes (19.6km) and continue into **Thwaite** on a short detour. The detour adds 0.5km to the route but allows a good view down Swaledale and a visit to the Kearton Hotel for food and drink in anticipation of the next climbs. Double back and turn right (20.1km) towards Hawes and the **Buttertubs**. The climb is less severe than that from Askrigg but still challenging with a false flat and final steep section to finish with.

Buttertubs

The Buttertubs are a series of 20m-deep fluted limestone potholes straddling the road. Possibly named after their shape, or because they were used to keep dairy products cool in summer.

The descent back to Wensleydale is well graded but with a few tight bends. Pass through Simonstone and turn right at the T-junction (29.1km) towards Hardraw and Sedbergh. Those who've had enough can turn left instead and return to Hawes having done half the distance and 629m of the climb.

At 30m Hardraw Force is the largest single drop waterfall in England. Access is via the Green Dragon Inn.

Pass through **Hardraw**. ◄ Turn right at the T-junction (30.9km) towards Sedbergh. The undulating road gradually ascends Mossdale. Pass the **Moorcock Inn** and its adjacent turn (37.4km) and continue towards Sedbergh. Pass under the Settle–Carlisle railway to **Garsdale Head**. Turn left (38.8km) to Garsdale Station. The following 2.75km climbs 225m, which is about as tough as it comes even though the climb is evenly graded. After peaking on Galloway Gate at 535m there follows an almost level section with fine views, descend into Dentdale. The road is well graded with some tight corners lower down. Pass Dent Station.

At 350m **Dent Station** is the highest railway station on the English network: first opened in 1877, it reopened in 1986.

Turn left at the T-junction (45.9km) in Lea Yeat to Hawes and Newby Head. Cross the river and start the riverside climb out of the valley. The climb is long but mostly gentle and the river a pleasing companion. Pass the Sportsman Inn before recrossing the river and continue up to and under the viaduct. The road steepens then levels before reaching **Newby Head**. Turn left at the T-junction (51.5km) for an undulating descent of **Widdale** on a wide road with good sight lines. Ignore all turns. Enter **Hawes**, turn right at the T-junction (62.0km) and pass through the main street to return to the start.

ROUTE 19
Semerwater

Start/Finish	National Park Visitor Centre car park east of the town centre SD 875 898
Distance	19.3km/12.1 miles
Total climb	350m
Grade	Short Challenging
Cycling time	1hr 5min
Café stops	Bainbridge

Fed by the waters of Cragdale, Raydale and Bardale, Semerwater lies above and aloof from Wensleydale. It is North Yorkshire's largest natural lake and the River Bain, at 3km, is England's shortest. Whichever way you approach there are significant climbs.

Turn left leaving the car park, heading east. Pass the turn (0.7km) for **Gayle**. Turn right (1.5km) to **Burtersett** for a short but steep climb. Climb through Burtersett as the road threads its way through. Bend left at the top as the road levels. Pass the left turn (2.2km). Shortly the road starts to climb, steeply at times. Well into the climb pass over the Roman Road (4.0km). Bend right (4.8km) and descend.

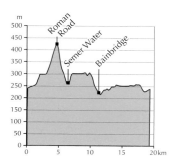

Semerwater

The descent is very steep in places and the bends can be tight so take care. Semerwater is soon revealed. Enter **Countersett**, turn right at the T-junction then immediately left (6.0km) towards Stalling Busk. Descend steeply to the shores of Semerwater.

> Those seeking a beautiful and tranquil Dales landscape of field barns and farmhouses may wish to take the road to **Marsett** signed from the Countersett junction. The byway from Marsett to Stalling Busk is more suited to a mountain bike. **Stalling Busk** is also worth a visit. The Wensleydale Triathlon swim is in Semerwater, with the bike route starting with the climb to Countersett.

Pass the gravel shore and climb away from the tarn. Turn left (7.2km) to Bainbridge. The road levels with the odd hill. Soon **Semerwater** is hidden from view by the gently rolling hills in the valley bottom. Start the descent (10.0km). Askrigg is visible ahead on the far side of the valley. Pass the turn (10.3km) for Carpley Green. As height is lost Bainbridge comes into view. Turn left at the T-junction with the main road (11.1km) and enter **Bainbridge** across the River Bain.

> **Bainbridge** is built around a large village green complete with stocks. Romans called it *Virosidum* and their fort is clearly visible to the east of town. There are waterfalls underneath the bridge.

Turn right on the village green (11.4km) towards Askrigg and cross the river. Turn left at the T-junction (12.2km) towards Hardraw. The remaining route is gently undulating with pleasant views over the dale. Pass the turn for **Sedbusk** (17.3km). Turn left (18.0km) to Hawes, cross the valley floor and the River Ure. Turn left at the T-junction in **Hawes** (19.3km) and left again to return to the start.

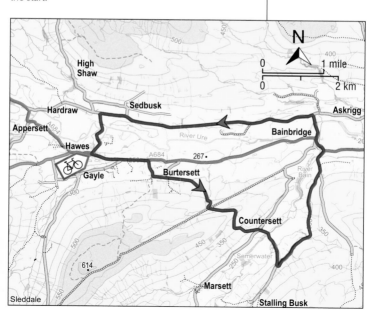

ROUTE 20
Coverdale and Langstrothdale Chase

Start/Finish	National Park Visitor Centre car park east of the town centre SD 875 898
Distance	70.7km/44.2 miles: alternative via Bishopsdale 50.9km/31.8 miles
Total climb	1175m: alternative via Bishopsdale 910m
Grade	Long Challenging
Cycling time	3hr 50min: alternative via Bishopsdale 2hr 45min
Café stops	Aysgarth, Kettlewell and Buckden

Three challenging climbs, each higher than the last, link four major dales. The first starts in West Witton after a pleasant ride down Wensleydale. The second is gentle until close to the top of Coverdale. The descent of Park Rash is steep but would be extremely challenging in the reverse direction. A gentle ride up Wharfedale and Langstrothdale leads to the Dales' highest road, Fleet Moss.

The Bishopdale option offers a substantial reduction in both distance and climb over the main route. Bishopsdale provides excellent cycling. Broad, level and fertile in its lower parts, it narrows and steepens as it reaches Kidstones Pass.

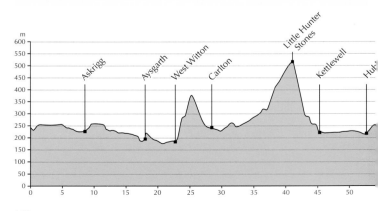

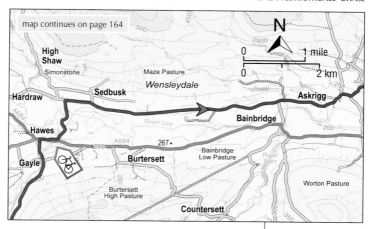

map continues on page 164

Turn right leaving the car park and immediately turn right again towards Hardraw and Muker. Cross the wide valley floor and cross the **River Ure**. After a short climb turn right (1.4km) towards Sedbusk and Askrigg. The undulating road heads down the dale on a shelf raised well above the river. Pass all side turns and enjoy the ride. Enter **Askrigg**.

For more information on **Askrigg** see the introduction to this chapter.

Climb the Main Street and bend right (9.3km) to Carperby. The climb continues, steep at times. After a right bend continue down the valley with only gentle climbs and descents. Pass through Nappa and **Woodhall**. Turn right approaching **Carperby** (15.8km) to Aysgarth and Aysgarth Falls. Descend to the river through Freeholders Wood. ▶

Here the sound of falling water can be heard.

163

Aysgarth Falls deserve being called a beauty spot. Three waterfalls are spread over 1.5km and connected by woodland walks. At the Upper Falls the River Ure cascades over a series of broad limestone steps and is the prettiest. A walk through Freeholders Wood leads to the Middle Falls which is the most spectacular.

Cross the river and climb steeply to the village of **Aysgarth**. Turn left at the T-junction (17.6km) to West Witton. Pass the turn (18.0km) for West Burton, unless taking the Bishopdale option.

Aysgarth Falls, Wensleydale

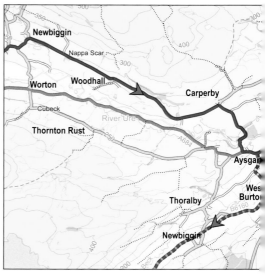

Alternative route via Bishopdale

Turn right towards West Burton and Kettlewell. Descend, pass the caravan site, bend left and cross Bishopdale Beck. Turn right at the T-junction (19.2km) towards Kettlewell and Grassington. Bend right (19.4km) and pass the turn for West Burton. Climb gently up the dale and pass the turns for Thoralby then Newbiggin (21.4km). The gradient remains gentle but increases after crossing the beck and passing New House Farm (25.9km). The gradient increases again on the approach to **Kidstones** (28.1km), where it is quite steep. The road peaks at 424m (29.5km). Descend, steeply at times with some tight bends and pass through **Cray** (31.6km). Turn right (32.1km) into an unsigned narrow lane and continue to descend. Turn right at the T-junction (32.6km), cross the stream and continue on a level section. Enter **Hubberholme**, bend left at the church and cross the river. Turn right at the T-junction by the George Inn (33.5km) to rejoin the main route at its 53.3km point.

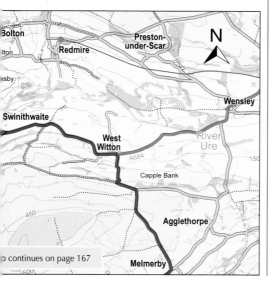

o continues on page 167

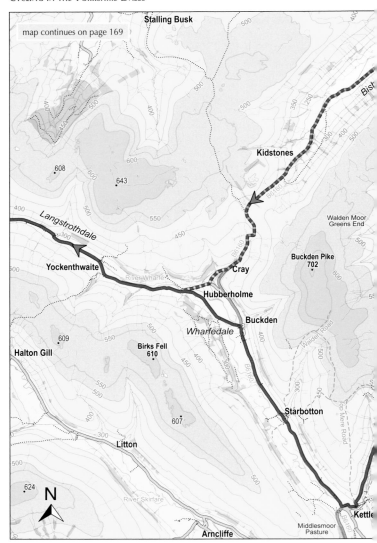

map continues on page 169

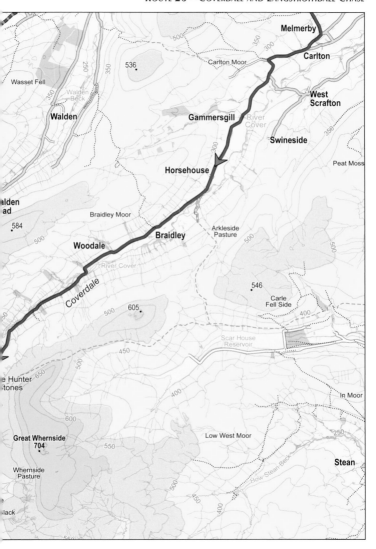

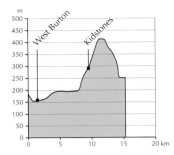

Pass through **Swinithwaite** and into **West Witton**. In West Witton turn right (23.4km) to Melmerby and Carlton. The climb is gentle at first but steepens considerably with a couple of sharp bends. These are followed by a diagonal climb up the dale side. Bend right as the climb eases by a junction (24.8km). Continue uphill, cross the open moor and descend into **Melmerby**. Turn right at the T-junction (27.4km) to Carlton and Kettlewell and right again (27.9km). Pass through the strung out village of **Carlton**.

Continue up Coverdale, with plenty of ups and downs which gradually gain height. Pass through **Gammersgill**, **Horsehouse**, **Braidley** and **Woodale** before crossing onto the south side of the dale by a popular picnic spot (37.4km). The climb to the head of the dale is relentless and often steep. The climb peaks at **Little Hunter Stones** 503m (41.7km). The descent is exhilarating. After an initial

*River Wharfe,
Langstrothdale*

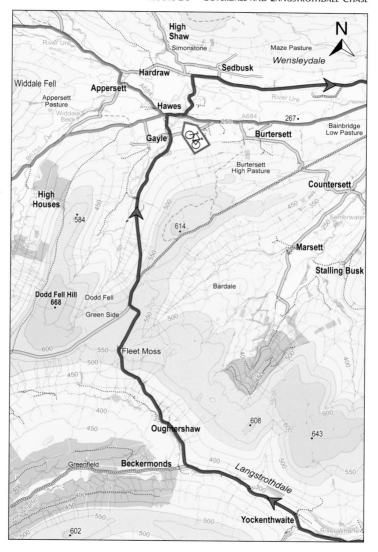

steep section the road levels before the very steep descent of **Park Rash** – beware as the bends are often gritty – into the pretty valley of Park Gill Beck. Approaching Kettlewell the road bends and steepens. Turn right at the T-junction (44.5km) and in **Kettlewell** right again at the crossroads (44.9km). Turn left at the village stores and turn right at the T-junction with the main road (46.1km).

Pass through **Starbotton**. In **Buckden** turn left (51.3km) to Hubberholme. This part of Wharfedale has steep sides and a wide flat valley floor which continues to **Hubberholme** where the dale divides. In Hubberholme climb away from the river and pass the George Inn (53.3km) where the Bishopdale option joins from the right. Continue the climb into Langstrothdale, descend through Raisgill and rejoin the river at **Yokenthwaite** (55.8km). Climb gently alongside the river that flows over a pitted limestone bed. Cross the river and climb away from the river. Bend right by a junction (59.1km) uphill to Hawes.

From **Oughtershaw** the climb is unrelenting but with a varying gradient. There are excellent views behind.

At 589m (63.9km) **Fleet Moss** is the highest road in Yorkshire.

Bend left, start to descend then bend right bend by an unsigned road junction (64.4km). Much of the descent of Sleddale has good sight lines. There are other vehicles and the road passes through working farms so take care. Enter **Gayle**, bend left over the river and descend into **Hawes**. Turn right at the T-junction with the main road (70.1km). Pass through the centre of town to return to the start.

Approaching Castle Bolton on Redmire Pasture (Route 22)

Located on a high shelf well away from the River Ure, Leyburn is the big town of Wensleydale. The River Ure is sometimes referred to as the Yore and Wensleydale was previously named Yoredale. Although lacking in a colourful history Leyburn is mentioned in the Domesday Book. Its charter was received in 1686 from Charles II and the market is still held on Fridays in the large market place. Leyburn also holds a Dales Food and Drinks Festival over the May Day weekend and an agricultural show in late August. The five main roads that meet here helped the town grow rapidly when the railway opened in 1856. To the east of town on the Shawl, good for views, there are remains of ancient British earthworks.

PARKING

There is ample car parking around the market square and in adjacent car parks.

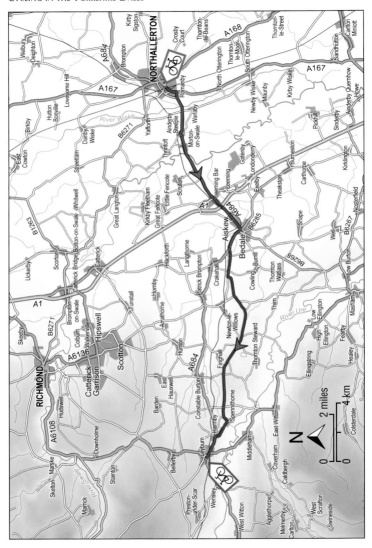

LINK ROUTE
Northallerton to Leyburn

Start	Northallerton railway station SE 364 932
Finish	Leyburn SE 111 905
Distance	28.8km/18 miles
Total climb	285m
Cycling time	1hr 20min
Café stops	Northallerton, Bedale and Leyburn

Turn right and leave Northallerton railway station. Pass under the railway bridge and cross the level crossing. Turn right at the roundabout (0.8km) to Bedale. Pass through **Ainderby Steeple**, complete with its church and village green, then through **Morton-on-Swale**. In **Leeming Bar** turn left at the mini-roundabout (8.9km) then bend right to Bedale. Pass under the motorway and enter **Aiskew**, which merges with **Bedale**. Continue straight ahead at the mini-roundabout. Descend, cross the railway then the river and bend left. Turn right at the T-junction (11.6km) and pass through the Market Place to leave Bedale.

Turn left (13.3km) towards Newton-le-Willows. Continue straight ahead at the two sets of crossroads then turn left (15.2km) into Moor End Lane. ▶ Turn left at the T-junction (16.7km) then right where the road bends left (17.3km) – in effect straight ahead. Pass the turn for Jervaulx Abbey then pass an unmarked one to the right and continue straight ahead at the crossroads (20.4km).

The route is undulating all the way to Leyburn.

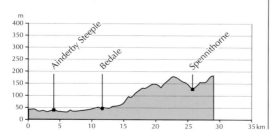

Approaching Fleet Moss, Langstrothdale far below (Route 20)

Pass an unmarked left turn then turn left at the T-junction (22.1km) to Spennithorne and continue straight ahead at the two sets of crossroads. Pass the turn for Leyburn (25.4km). Turn right in **Spennithorne** (25.9km) to Harmby and Leyburn. Climb through **Harmby** and turn left at the T-junction (27.2km) to Leyburn. Enter **Leyburn**. Pass the turn for Middleham and Ripon. Climb into town and at the far end of the market square is the roundabout.

ROUTE 21
Swaledale and the Fleak

Start/Finish	The roundabout, western end of the market square SE 111 905
Distance	44.8km/28 milies
Total climb	765m
Grade	Medium Challenging
Cycling time	2hr 25min
Café stops	Fremington (The Dales Bike Centre) and Reeth. Close to the route there are cafés in Askrigg and Bolton Castle

High moors and verdant dales in equal measure. The defining feature though is climbing The Fleak at 544m. It is high but the gradient up is not even; there are several brutish sections. The descent back into Wensleydale is also steep and proved decisive in one of the early Tour of Britain Cycle Races. There is one short option that keeps to the south side of Swaledale. It is described in the text rather than given a section of its own.

Take the road north from the roundabout towards Richmond. Turn left (0.1km) to Grinton and Reeth. Climb steeply out of town and pass the quarries and industrial unit on the left. The gradient soon eases and the town is left behind. Continue straight ahead at the crossroads (2.9km) to Grinton and Reeth. Heather moors bound the road, which continues to climb. Pass the army ranges on one side and mine scarred grouse moors on the other. Cross the watershed at **Robin Cross** 420m (6.8km). Descend with views over Reeth and Swaledale. ▶ Pass Grinton Lodge Youth Hostel. Pass the turn (10.5km) for Redmire and descend steeply into **Grinton**. The left turn alongside the churchyard (11.25km) is the start of the Harkerside option. Otherwise continue straight ahead and turn left at the T-junction by the Bridge Inn (11.3km) to Reeth.

Beware of sharp bends and hidden drops.

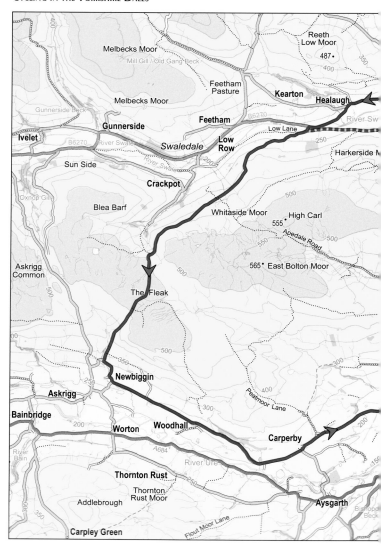

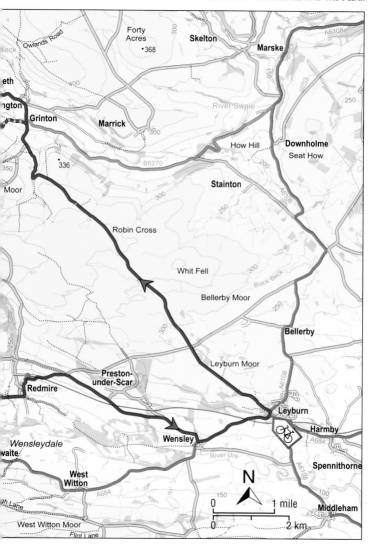

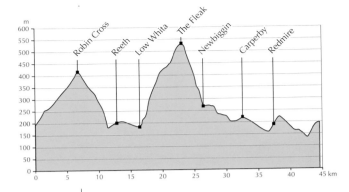

Harkerside option

If you have no need to visit Reeth, enjoy quiet roads and want to practice steep climbs this is for you.

◄ It has a little more climb but cuts 0.7km from the main route. Turn left to Harkerside on the lane beside the churchyard. Leave Grinton and climb steeply before a descent through open pasture. At the right turn (15.6km) for Reeth rejoin the main route and continue straight ahead towards Askrigg.

Harkerside, Swaledale

Leave Grinton, cross the River Swale, pass through **Fremington**, cross Arkle Beck and climb into **Reeth**. Pass through Reeth and leave the village green (12.8km) towards Gunnerside. Climb steeply out of town. Pass through **Healaugh**. Turn left (16.1km) to Askrigg and cross the River Swale at Low Whita. Turn right at the T-junction (16.2km) towards Askrigg. ▶ The climb to The Fleak, some 355m above, is mostly on unenclosed roads. The gradient alternates between steep sections of varying lengths followed by flatter sections and the odd dip. The road signs never indicate more than 20 per cent, which contradicts the Ordnance Survey map. Heather takes over from grass. **The Fleak** at 544m (23.0km) is unmarked. The descent starts at a cattle grid and is very steep at times. Straight ahead Semerwater in Raydale is clearly visible. Turn left at the minor unmarked junction with the grass triangle (25.8km). Continue downhill and pass through **Newbiggin**. Turn left at the T-junction (26.4km). Continue down the dale, with only gentle climbs and descents. Pass through Nappa and **Woodhall**. In **Carperby** (32.2km) pass the turn for Aysgarth.

Descent into Wensleydale, Semerwater and Raydale visible on the left

This is where the Harkerside option rejoins the main route.

Climbing the Fleak, grit and determination required

Pass the turn for Castle Bolton (35.9km) and continue into **Redmire** on the main road. Bend left to Leyburn, climb through and out of the village. Pass under the railway and pass the turn for Redmire Station. Pass the turn for Richmond and gently descend into **Wensley**. Turn left at the T-junction in Wensley (42.7km) to Leyburn on a relatively busy road. A final climb ends at the start roundabout in **Leyburn**.

ROUTE 22

Aysgarth Falls

Start/Finish	The roundabout, western end of the market square SE 111 905
Distance	26.9km/16.8 miles
Total climb	360m
Grade	Short Hard
Cycling time	1hr 25min
Café stops	Bolton Castle and Aysgarth

A short and pleasant cycle ride through lower Wensleydale, taking in Bolton Castle and Aysgarth Falls. Ideal for a social trip with cameras and picnics at the ready. For those seeking something more it is easily combined with Route 23.

Take the road north from the roundabout towards Richmond. Turn left (0.1km) to Grinton and Reeth. Climb steeply out of town and pass the quarries and industrial unit on the left. The gradient soon eases and the town is left behind. Turn left at the crossroads (2.9km) towards Redmire and Carperby. The road climbs, dips, then climbs again to the top of **Redmire Scar** (5.5km) before a sweeping descent through Scarlet Wood with

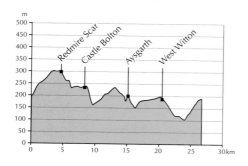

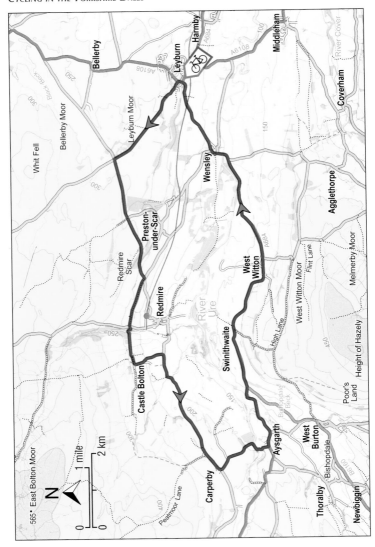

Bolton Castle, Castle Bolton, Wensleydale

views up Wensleydale and across into Bishopdale and Waldendale. Turn right at the T-junction (6.4km) towards Redmire and immediately turn right again onto a narrow lane with grass growing along its centre. Only a Yorkshire Dales Cycleway sign gives it away. This gated lane has good views of the dale with Bolton Castle ahead. After a final gate continue straight ahead at the staggered cross-roads (7.8km) to **Castle Bolton**.

The fortified manor house of **Bolton Castle** dominates Castle Bolton. It has been unoccupied since the Civil War, when the defending Royalists were reduced to eating horseflesh. Its most famous occupant was Mary Queen of Scots, whose unpopularity at home had forced her to abdicate and seek refuge in England. Today the castle is owned by the same family that built it and is open to the public.

Bend left at the castle and descend. Turn right at the T-junction (9.8km) to Carperby. Pass through **Carperby** and turn left (13.5km) to Aysgarth and Aysgarth Falls. Descend to the river through Freeholders Wood. ◄

Here the sound of falling water can be heard.

> **Aysgarth Falls** deserve being called a beauty spot. Three waterfalls are spread over 1.5km and are connected by woodland walks. At the Upper Falls – the prettiest – the River Ure cascades over a series of broad limestone steps. A walk through Freeholders Wood leads to the Middle Falls, which is the most spectacular.

Cross the river and climb steeply to the village of **Aysgarth**. Turn left at the T-junction (15.3km) to West Witton and Leyburn. Pass the turn for West Burton. Pass through **Swinithwaite** and **West Witton** as the road wends its way along the dale side. Descend and cross the River Ure. Pass through **Wensley** for a final climb which ends at the start roundabout in **Leyburn**.

ROUTE 23

Jervaulx Abbey and Middleham

Start/Finish	The roundabout, western end of the market square SE 111 905
Distance	23.9km/14.9 miles
Total climb	205m
Grade	Short Moderate
Cycling time	1hr 5min
Café stops	Jervaulx and Middleham

Quite possibly the easiest route in this guidebook. The first half is through gently rolling farmland, in complete contrast to the other rides. The return visits Jervaulx Abbey and the village of Middleham.

Take the road east and slightly downhill from the roundabout towards Bedale and Northallerton. Pass the turn for Ripon (0.5km). Turn right opposite the Pheasant Inn (1.8km) to Harmby and Spennithorne. Pass through **Harmby** and after a short section of fields enter **Spennithorne**. Turn left at the T-junction (3.1km) towards Finghall. Continue straight ahead at the two sets of crossroads (4.2km and 6.5km). ▶

Turn right (7.0km) towards Newton-le-Willows and Bedale. Continue straight ahead at the crossroads (8.8km).

The road is wide and gently undulating.

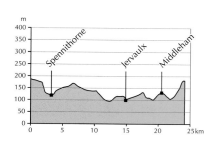

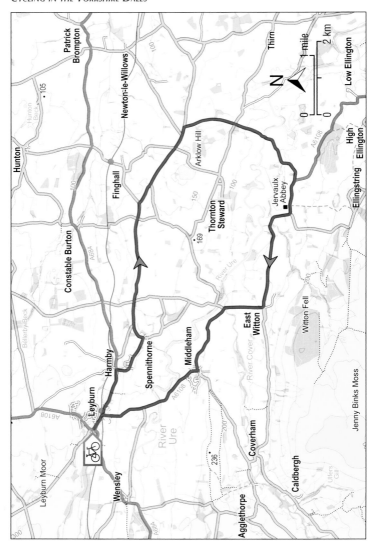

Turn right opposite Cocked Hat farm (9.5km) onto an unsigned road. Continue straight ahead at the crossroads (10.9km) to Jervaulx. Cross the Ure, after which the road narrows and becomes twistier. Turn right at the T-junction with the main road (13.4km) to Middleham and Leyburn. On the right the walled Jervaulx Park contains the ruined abbey. The entrance to **Jervaulx Abbey** is opposite the tearooms (14.7km).

> **Jervaulx Abbey** was established by Cistercian monks in 1156. The ground plans can be easily followed but its real beauty can only be hinted at from what remains standing. The Dissolution of the Monasteries in the 1530s saw its closure. Now in private hands, it is open daily.

Bend right in **East Witton** (17.3km) and descend to the river. Cross the River Cover at Cover Bridge (18.3km) and bend left at the Cover Inn to Leyburn. Climb gently to **Middleham**.

Scenic but not hilly

Formerly the capital of Wensleydale, **Middleham** was famous for its markets and fairs. The much reduced castle was once owned by Richard III and was made unusable after the Civil War since when it has been used as a ready source for building materials. Today Middleham is best known as one of the country's top race horse training and breeding centres; something that may date back to the days of Jervaulx Abbey.

Bend right in the village square (20.4km) to Leyburn. Descend and cross the Ure. Climb, gently at first, into **Leyburn**. Turn left by the petrol station (23.4km) towards Hawes and return to the start.

TOUR DE FRANCE 2014

Looking back up Swaledale from Reeth

In December 2012 it was announced that the *Grand Départ* of the 101st Tour de France would be hosted by Yorkshire. Stage 1 from Leeds to Harrogate visits the Yorkshire Dales. Stage 2 is from York to Sheffield and Stage 3 from Cambridge to London.

Stage 1 is just over 200km long, including some steep climbs and descents. It is described here in full as a single day ride for strong cyclists with good stamina, who want to test themselves against their TdeF heroes. It can also be made into a slightly shorter circular route starting in Harrogate, joining the route in Wharfedale and avoiding the urban section in Leeds, and that variant is also described below. If you decide to make a long weekend of it, you'll find plenty of accommodation in Grassington near to Threshfield, Hawes and Reeth along the route. See Appendix B for details of Tourist Information Centres.

It is not possible to cycle every metre in the tracks of the professionals as one early section is on private roads and the finish would be against the traffic on a one way street. Where there are variations they are explained below.

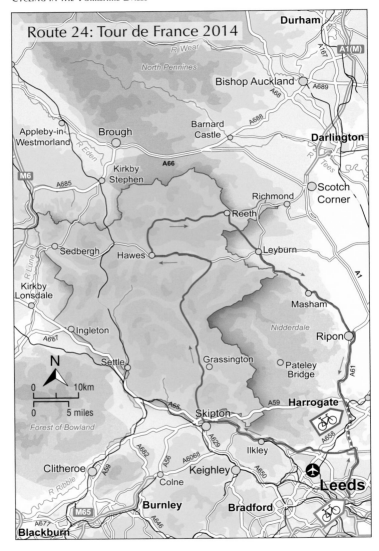

ROUTE 24

Tour de France 2014
Stage 1: Leeds to Harrogate

Start	Leeds Town Hall, The Headrow, Leeds SE 297 338
Alternative Start/Finish	A659 and A61 junction, Harewood Bridge SE 312 457
Finish	The War Memorial, West Park, Harrogate SE 301 555
Distance	205.8km/128.6 miles: variant loop 201.4km/125.9 miles
Total climb	2125m: variant loop 2030m
Grade	Long Moderate
Cycling time	9hr 55min: variant loop 9hr 40min
Café stops	Otley, Ilkley, Skipton, Cracoe, Kettlewell, Buckden, Aysgarth, Bainbridge, Hawes, Thwaite (Kearton Country Hotel), Muker, Gunnerside, Reeth, Fremington (The Dales Bike Centre), Leyburn, Middleham, Jervaulx, Masham (Bordar House Teas is the cyclists' café) and Ripon
Public transport	Leeds Town Hall is 500m from the city's railway station and is included on the inset map of Leeds centre. Harrogate's is 250m from the finish on West Park. Services between the two stations are run by Northern Rail and East Coast. Northern Rail runs up to four trains an hour at peak and two per hour at off peak times. Up to two cycles can be carried per train but reservations are not possible. East Coast runs an early morning train from Harrogate to London which stops in Leeds. The return service arrives in Harrogate in the evening. Up to five cycles can be carried and spaces must be reserved in advance. A tandem counts as two cycles
Car parks	Both Leeds and Harrogate have a number of multi-storey car parks close to their centres most of which close over night. In addition to lower charges Harrogate also has ground level long stay car parks which are accessible all day as well as free on street parking within a short distance of the town centre. A useful website is en.parkopedia.co.uk.

This route is a long, strenuous, rewarding ride in the Yorkshire Dales and is a rare opportunity to share something with the professionals. The first half of the ride includes the contrasting dales of Wharfedale and Bishopdale in almost their entirety, experiencing the gradual changes in the natural and man-made landscapes. The Aysgarth–Hawes section is Wensleydale at its best. Swaledale is a contrast, enclosed by steep hillsides with timeless villages and a road that is never straight nor level nor wide. As Harrogate approaches the roads straighten and the climbs ease. There are three significant climbs on the route, Kidstones, Buttertubs and out of Grinton, each with its own challenges and character. The spa town of Harrogate is a good choice as finish. A popular destination in its own right, it has everything the recuperating cyclist could need.

The variant, avoiding the centre of Leeds and creating a loop back to Harewood Bridge, 14.8km out from Leeds, changes the route from a point-to-point into a loop, but does nothing to alter its overall nature. It eliminates the logistic challenge of transfers between Leeds and Harrogate. There is a reduction in distance of 4.4km. The road can be very busy, but no more so than the urban section in Leeds.

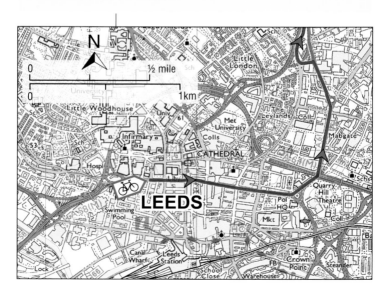

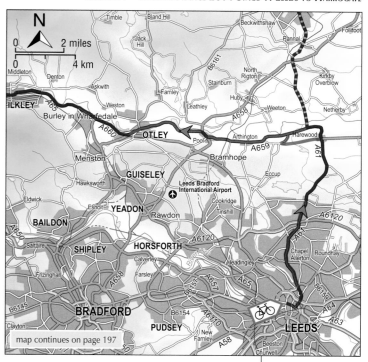

Leave the Town Hall, heading east on the Headrow and continue straight ahead at all junctions. After a gentle descent take the second exit at the roundabout with the fountains (0.9km) towards Harrogate on the A61. Pass under the motorway. At the roundabout with the trees (1.6km) bend slightly left and continue towards Harrogate. Bend left with the road and move into the right hand lane. At this point the Tour will continue straight ahead to cut through the one way system. Continue straight ahead at the junction, immediately bend right and move into the left hand lane. At the next junction continue straight ahead and again bend right keeping to the left hand lane (2.1km). Follow the signs towards Harrogate on the A61. Continue on this road as it climbs to Alwoodley. The dual carriageway ends at a roundabout (8.9km) on the northern edge of Leeds. Descend then climb to **Harewood**. Continue straight ahead at the traffic lights (13.2km) towards Harrogate. Here the Tour will turn left through the arch to pass by Harewood House.

Construction of the stately home of **Harewood House**, a Grade 1 listed building, took from 1759 to 1771 for Edwin Lascelles, who made his money

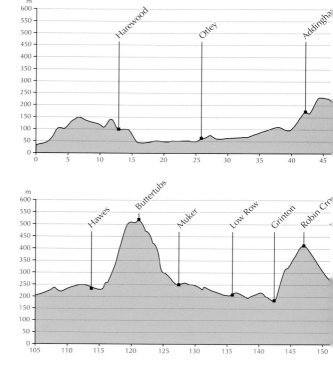

in the West Indies. Capability Brown did the land-
scaping. The house is pronounced 'Harwood' but
the village 'Hairwood'. The estate is home of the set
for the popular television drama series *Emmerdale*.

Descend and sweep left into Wharfedale. Turn left
to Arthington, Pool and Otley where the Harrogate road
bends right (14.8km). The Tour rejoins the route on this
straight section. Pass through **Arthington** and enter **Pool**.
Turn right at the roundabout (21.9km) and left before the
petrol station (22.5km) to Otley and Skipton. Continue on

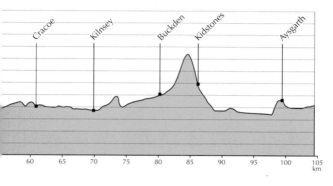

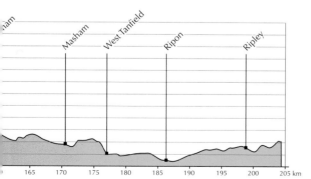

this level road into **Otley**. Approaching Otley the southern skyline is dominated by the wooded ridge of the Chevin.

> Although there is evidence of Bronze Age activity in Wharfedale, **Otley** really started to grow in Saxon times: it gained its market charter in 1222 from Henry III. The market continues on Fridays. The small-scale woollen industry boomed with industrialisation and many of the mills still exist. Its most famous son was Thomas Chippendale, the cabinet maker, and its most famous daughter is Lizzie Armitstead, the cyclist. JMW Turner visited in 1797 and in his *Hannibal* painting the Alps look very similar to the Chevin.

It is at this point that the Link Route Leeds Bradford Airport–Askwith crosses the route.

Pass the market square and continue straight ahead at the staggered crossroads controlled by traffic lights (26.9km) to Ilkley and Skipton. ◄ Turn right at the roundabout (27.8km) towards Skipton. Continue straight ahead at the next two roundabouts to Skipton and bypass **Burley in Wharfedale**. Pass through the centre of **Ilkley** (37.0km) and continue towards Skipton.

Wharfedale from the Chevin

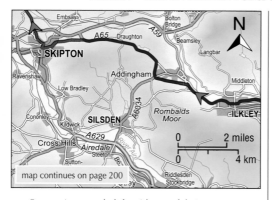

map continues on page 200

Bronze Age people left evidence of their presence on **Ilkley Moor**, which overlooks the town, in the form of hundreds of rock carvings which include cup and ring markings as well as the Swastika Stone. The Romans had a military station here but it was the exploitation in the 17th and 18th centuries of medicinal spring waters that lead to a Victorian boom for the town.

Today it is an elegant floral town popular with visitors who enjoy the many tea shops or the pleasure of walking or rock climbing on Ilkley Moor, on which the song 'On Ilkla Moor Baht 'at' is based.

Climb gently out of Ilkley, descent towards the river then climb round and above **Addingham**. Continue straight ahead at the roundabout (42.8km) towards Skipton. Continue the climb to Chelker Reservoir (45.3km). Leave Wharfedale and enter Airedale. Descend and pass the turns for **Draughton**.

Turn left (49.4km) signed 'Skipton local traffic'. Pass under the railway line and descend into **Skipton**. Turn right at the mini-roundabout (52.0km). At the next roundabout in the centre of town turn right into the High Street. Turn left at the roundabout with the memorial (52.4km) towards Settle, Kendal and Grassington. Climb out of

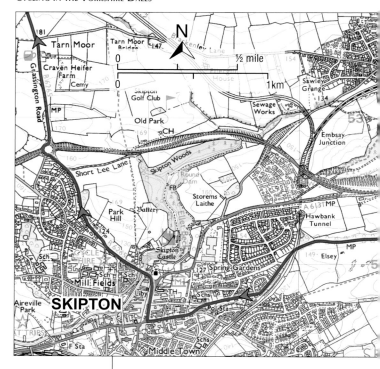

Skipton and continue straight ahead at the roundabout on the bypass (53.6km) towards Grassington.

Today **Skipton** is a prosperous market town with a name derived from the Old English *sceaptun* ('sheep town'). The wide High Street was used for cattle and sheep markets, which continue at a modern market to the west of town. The first castle was built in the 11th century and has been rebuilt since. The industrial revolution brought mills, the railway and a canal.

After the initial climb out of Skipton the route undulates without any significant climbs all the way to Buckden. Take in the views of Flasby Fell to the west and Embsay Moor, Rylstone and Cracoe Fells to the east. Pass through **Rylstone** (60.1km).

It was the Rylstone and District Women's Institute's saucy fundraising calendar that inspired the film **Calendar Girls** and every group, apart from a few enclosed orders, to do the same. Not so widely copied was turning the village green into a duck pond.

Pass through **Cracoe** (61.6km), bend left, pass the quarry, pass the turn for Linton, descend into **Threshfield** (65.4km) and return to Wharfedale. Pass through the village, pass the turn for Grassington (65.7km) and continue to Kettlewell, with the River Wharfe as company for much of the time. Pass through **Kilnsey** (70.4km) and under Kilnsey Crag, a 50m rock face with a 10m overhang that attracts rock climbers by the score. Bend right to pass the turn for Arncliffe and Litton (71.5km), cross the River Skirfare and climb away from the valley bottom for a short elevated section. Descend on a sweeping right bend, cross the River Wharfe and enter **Kettlewell** (75.4km).

Pass through the village towards Buckden and Aysgarth. ▶ Pass through **Starbotton** then **Buckden** (81.0km) towards Aysgarth and Hawes. The climb out

The dale is wide and the cycling easy.

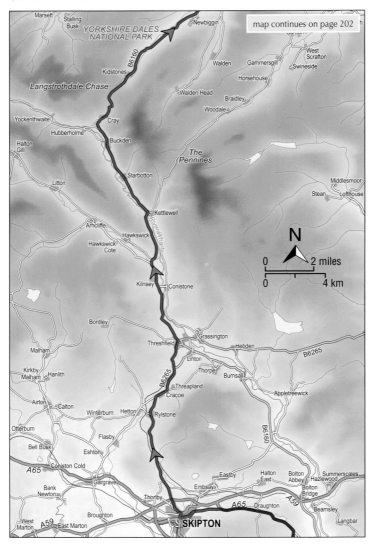

map continues on page 202

Bishopdale, approaching Kidstones

of Wharfedale starts gently but steepens where the road bends right, before easing in the lovely valley of Cray Gill, with its many waterfalls. The road will steepen and ease many times on the ascent. Pass through **Cray** (83.5km). A final steep section ends with a level section (84.1km), although the highest point at 424m (85.4km) is a little way off.

Descend into Bishopdale. With gentle gradients, good sight lines and a wide road the descent of Bishopdale is a delight. Climb then pass the Street Head Inn (93.2km) and in the dip pass the turn for Thoralby (93.5km). Continue down the dale. Pass the turn for West Burton then pass the turn for 'Aysgarth 2 miles' (95.7km). Turn left at the T-junction (97.6km) to Aysgarth and Hawes. Cross Bishopdale Beck and climb to Aysgarth in Wensleydale. Pass the turn for the waterfalls, bend right at the petrol station (100.4km) and pass through the remainder of the village to Hawes.

Aysgarth Falls deserves to be called a beauty spot. Three waterfalls are spread over 1.5km and are connected by woodland walks. At the Upper Falls – the

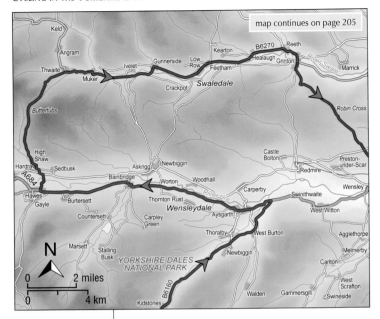

map continues on page 205

prettiest – the River Ure cascades over a series of broad limestone steps. A walk through Freeholders Wood leads to the Middle Falls, which is the most spectacular.

Descend towards the river and continue on this undulating and sinuous main road. Pass through **Worton** (105.7km). Bend right, descend, cross the River Bain and enter **Bainbridge** (108.0km). Cross the village green to Hawes. Turn left at the T-junction (108.3km) again to Hawes.

Bainbridge is built around a large village green complete with stocks. Romans called it *Virosidum* and their fort is clearly visible to the east of town. There are waterfalls underneath the bridge.

The road now undulates a little more but curves a little less. In **Hawes** (114.3km) turn right at the sculpture of the shepherd and sheep towards Hardraw and Muker.

Hawes has been a market town since it got its charter in 1699. The market continues every Tuesday. Its name derives from Old Norse and means 'pass between the mountains'. Hawes is a popular spot for visitors and is nearly always busy. There are several museums and the Wensleydale Creamery, with visitor centre, to visit.

Leave Hawes, cross the River Ure, climb away from the wide dale floor and turn left at the T-junction (115.7km) towards Hardraw and Muker. Turn right at the next junction (116.0km) uphill to Simonstone and Muker. Pass through Simonstone, after which the gradient increases, with some challenging sections, the final one easing at a cattle grid (118.3km). The climb continues less severely, with the bulk of Shunner Fell dominating the western skyline. From the high point at 526m (120.9km) descend steeply into Swaledale and pass the **Buttertubs**.

The **Buttertubs** are a series of 20m-deep fluted limestone potholes straddling the road, possibly named after their shape or because they were used to keep dairy products cool in summer.

Continue on the level section built into the steep hillside, climb over the shallow spur and descend steeply again taking care at the bends. Turn right at the T-junction (124.8km) towards Muker and Richmond. A left turn to Thwaite adds 0.5km to the route, allows a good views down Swaledale and a visit to the excellent Kearton Hotel for food and drink. The narrow road down the dale has many small climbs, with numerous bends, and the trees reduce the sightlines. Pass through **Muker** (126.5km). Pass through **Gunnerside** (131.1km) towards Reeth and Richmond. Pass through **Low Row**, **Feetham**, climb through **Healaugh** and descend into **Reeth** (140.8km).

Gunnerside with Gunnerside Gill behind, Swaledale

Few settlements have a location such as that enjoyed by **Reeth**, spread over a south-facing slope and sheltered by hills to the north: sitting above the River Swale, and upstream from its confluence with Arkle Beck, Reeth's aspect is best revealed when approaching from the south.

Originally a Saxon settlement, Reeth was important enough to be included in the Domesday Book. Lead was mined before the Romans came and this continued until just over a century ago. The marks remain to be seen and visited in the surrounding hills. The town got its market charter in 1695.

Cross the green and leave Reeth towards Leyburn and Richmond. Cross Arkle Beck and pass through Fremington. Cross the River Swale and enter **Grinton**. Turn right (141.3km) where the road bends left at the Bridge Inn, towards Leyburn and Redmire. The road is narrow and climbs steeply alongside the wooded Grinton Gill. Beyond the cattle grid the gradient eases and unenclosed moorland takes over. Pass the turn (143.0km) for Redmire then pass the youth hostel at Grinton Lodge. The climb of Grinton Moor is sustained, with a varying gradient. At the high point, 420m (146.6km), the road becomes enclosed, with an army training area on one side and the mine-scarred Preston Moor on the other. The descent is a pleasure, with gentle gradients and good sight lines. After a short climb continue straight ahead at the crossroads (150.5km) to Leyburn. The descent resumes and steepens on entering **Leyburn**. Turn right at the T-junction (153.4km) towards Hawes and Ripon, then left at the roundabout (153.6km) towards Northallerton, Bedale and Ripon. Pass the market square and turn right at the petrol station (153.9km) to Middleham and Ripon.

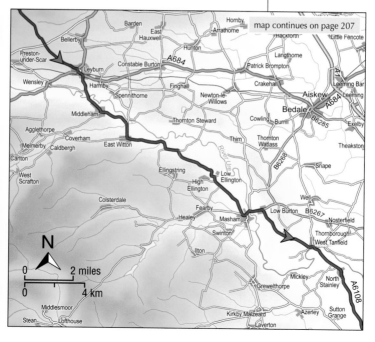

map continues on page 207

Located on a high shelf well away from the River Ure, **Leyburn** is the big town of Wensleydale. The River Ure is sometimes referred to as the Yore, and Wensleydale was previously named Yoredale. Although lacking in a colourful history Leyburn is mentioned in the Domesday Book. Its charter was received in 1686 from Charles II and the market is still held on Fridays. Leyburn also holds a Dales Food and Drinks Festival over the May Day weekend and an agricultural show in late August. The five main roads that meet here helped the town grow rapidly, and the railway opened in 1856. To the east of town on the Shawl, good for views, there are remains of ancient British earthworks.

The River Ure is crossed several times.

This road leads all the way to Ripon. As progress is made the undulations decrease and the road becomes straighter. ◄ Descend, cross the River Ure and climb to **Middleham**. Turn left in the square (157.0km) to Ripon.

Formerly the capital of Wensleydale, **Middleham** was famous for its markets and fairs. The much reduced castle was once owned by Richard III and was made unusable after the Civil War, since when it has been used as a ready source for building materials. Today Middleham is best known as one of the country's top racehorse training and breeding centres, something that may date back to the days of Jervaulx Abbey.

Jervaulx Abbey was established by Cistercian monks in 1156. The ground plans can be easily followed, but its real beauty can only be hinted at from what remains standing. The dissolution of the Monasteries in the 1530s saw its closure. Now in private hands, it is open daily.

Descend and this time cross the River Cover, climb to **East Witton** and bend left. Pass through Jervaulx and on to **Masham** (170.8km).

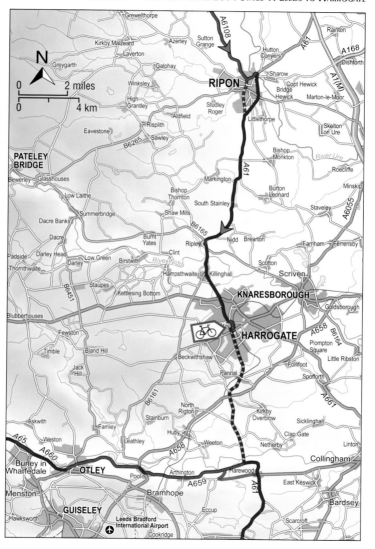

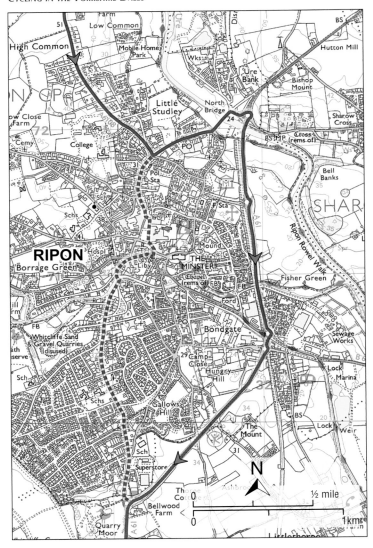

The road skirts the north side of town. Continue to Ripon. Turn right at the roundabout in **West Tanfield** (176.7km), again to Ripon. Pass through **North Stainley** (179.3km) and enter **Ripon** (184.7km). Turn left at the Clock Tower junction, cross the River Ure, turn right at the mini-roundabout then turn right at the large roundabout on the city's bypass (185.6km) to Harrogate.

To see something of **Ripon** turn right at the Clock Tower junction to the city centre. Continue straight ahead at the traffic lights, then keep left as the road divides and enter the city square. Fork left at the end of the square towards the hospital, bend right, descend, then turn right at the T-junction, again towards the hospital. Turn left at the traffic lights into Low Skellgate, which becomes Harrogate Road south of the river. Continue straight ahead on this road and at the roundabout join the main route at the fourth roundabout to Harrogate.

Ripon's history dates from 672, when Saint Wilfrid dedicated a church to Saint Peter, over the ruins of which the Gothic cathedral was built. It received its

Entrance to Ripon Cathedral

charter of incorporation in 886 from Alfred the Great, and its market charter in 1108. The market continues every Thursday. At 9pm each night the Hornblower performs his official duties in the square to maintain the 1300-year-old unbroken tradition. The duties were originally performed by the wakeman, who had powers similar to a mayor. The city has many medieval and Georgian buildings, a racecourse and is at the northern end of the canal network.

Cross the River Ure for the final time. At 20m above sea level this is the lowest point on the ride. From here to the end the road is usually busy with speeding traffic. Continue straight ahead at the next three roundabouts and turn left at the fourth on the southern side of the city to Harrogate. Pass through Wormald Green and **South Stainley**. Turn left at the roundabout in **Ripley** (199.0km) and straight ahead at the next. Cross the River Nidd and pass through **Killinghall** (201.2km).

Enter **Harrogate** and continue straight ahead at the roundabout (203.1km) to the town centre. Pass the Hydro **swimming pool** and climb, before descending to the **Royal Hall Theatre**. Here the Tour de France race route continues straight ahead up Parliament Street for a sprint finish on West Park. This is a one-way street, however, so turn left at the traffic lights (204.7km) towards Leeds. Move to the middle lane and turn right at the next set of lights, keeping in the right hand lane again towards Leeds. Climb Cheltenham Parade and bend left to pass the bus station. Pass the railway station, continue straight ahead at the traffic lights and turn next right into Raglan Street. The T-junction at the end of Raglan Street with West Park is the location of the finish of Stage 1 of the Tour de France 2014. Turn right and shortly arrive at the **war memorial** (205.8km) to reach the end of the route.

The first reference to **Harrogate** dates from the 14th century. It was the discovery of a mineral spring in 1571 that saw it grow as a spa town. Today it is an elegant and genteel conference and visitor centre.

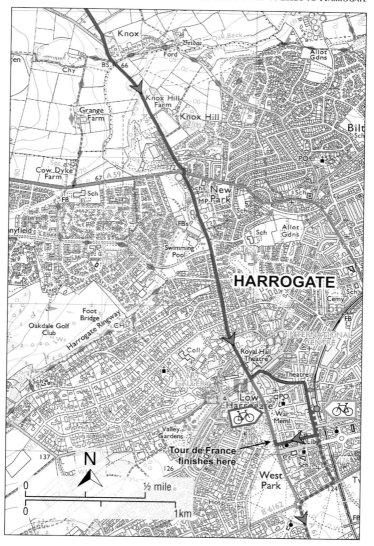

Tour de France
finishes here

The war memorial, West Park, Harrogate

It is proud if its floral tradition, with the Valley Gardens and RHS Harlow Carr being of particular note. To west, south and east of the town centre lies the Stray, 200 acres of unenclosed parkland protected by Parliament for all to enjoy.

Variant to loop back to Harewood Bridge

Leave Harrogate railway station and turn left, following the one way system. Continue straight ahead at the first and second sets of traffic lights. At the third stay in the left hand lane but turn right towards Leeds on the A61. From this point the route continues towards Leeds on the A61. Turn left at the roundabout and cross the Stray. Continue straight ahead at all roundabouts and traffic lights from here on. Descend and leave Harrogate. Cross Crimple Beck then pass through **Pannal** (4.1km). Continue straight ahead at the bypass (5.7km) and soon the gentle descent into Wharfedale starts. Ahead lie the wooded slopes of the Harewood estate. Cross the River Wharfe at Harewood Bridge (10.1km) and turn right where the road bends left (10.4km) to Otley, Pool and Addingham. Rejoin the main route at its 14.8km point.

LA VUELTA A DALES

Approaching Park Rash, Wharfedale (Stage 3)

Start/Finish	Settle
Distance	305km/203 miles
Climb	4345m
Grade	Medium Hard to Long Challenging

A multi-day cycling immersion in the Yorkshire Dales. The route is described in six stages starting in Settle but riders should feel free to select their own start point, pace and distances. Cycle camping is the ideal way to get close to the landscapes and nature of the area and to really experience the Dales in all of its moods. Camping equipment will add 20 to 30 per cent to the cycling times given but will increase the satisfaction of a challenge well met.

Details of campsites on or close to the route have been listed in Appendix C. Bed and breakfast and hotel accommodation is plentiful. The National Park and Tourist Information centres listed in Appendix B will be able to provide uptodate information.

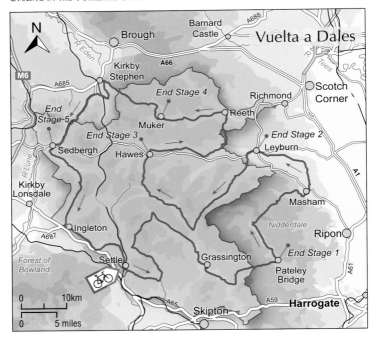

If you choose to do any of these stages individually, you will need to find a way to get back from your finish point to the start. There are no public transport options that could turn any stage into a day ride. If you are able to arrange a lift back to a parked car, the parking options at the start point of each stage are described below.

STAGE 1
Settle to Pateley Bridge

Start	Whitefriars Court car park SD 819 638
Finish	Low Wath Road SE 156 654
Distance	71.2km/44.5 miles
Total climb	1030m
Grade	Long Hard
Cycling time	3hr 40min
Café stops	Malham (The Old Barn on the main road and Beck Hall signed off Cove Road), Grassington, Burnsall, Stump Cross Caverns and Pateley Bridge
Parking at start	The three council-run car parks in Settle are fine for daily use but they do not permit parking for more than 23 hours in a 24-hour period. Multi-day continuous stays are not possible, even with their seven-day ticket. There is plenty of free and unrestricted on-street parking not far from the town centre which will not impose on residents.

Two challenging climbs reveal the finest of karst landscapes, particularly that around Attermire Scar and Malham Cove. A climb over Dale Head, with high fells either side, leads to Littondale and Wharfedale for a gentle ride in two fine limestone dales. From Appletreewick a final challenging climb and tricky descent ends in Nidderdale.

SETTLE

Settle's history can be traced back to the 7th century. In 1249 it got its market charter and the market continues every Tuesday. Cotton spinning started in the late 18th century, harnessing the power of the River Ribble. The Settle–Carlisle railway opened in 1875. The Naked Man café dates back to 1663, making it possibly the oldest in the country.

Turn right leaving the car park. Turn left (0.2km) and diagonally cross the square towards Airton. Turn left at the

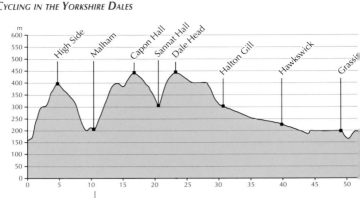

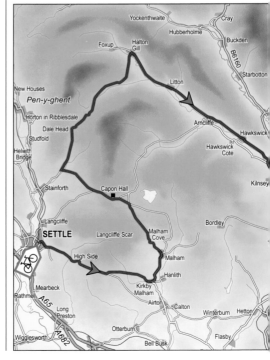

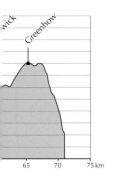

T-junction (0.4km), bend right then fork right in front of the large Elizabethan style manor house towards Kirkby Malham and Airton. Pass over the cobbles and start the climb. Bend left (0.6km) uphill. Pass the junction (0.8km) and continue uphill. The climb is very steep in places, and the lane narrows, but does eventually ease (1.5km). To the left limestone scars dominate the skyline.

Attermire Scar is one of several that cut into and mark the southern and western sides of the limestone hill of **Langcliffe Scar**. The scars are caused by the Craven Fault. At the western end, Victoria Cave has yielded mammoth, bear, hippopotamus,

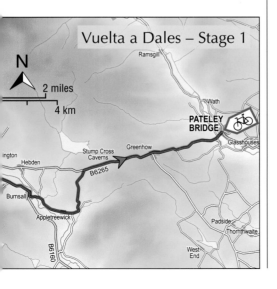

Malham

rhinoceros and reindeer remnants, plus man-made artefacts dating back to the last interglacial period.

Pass the stile (2.8km), unless a visit to Scaleber Force is called for. After a quick dip, the climb, steep in sections, resumes. Cross the cattle grid (4.4km) onto unenclosed grass-covered moor. Bend left (5.5km) to Kirkby Malham by the turn for Airton. Cross the cattle grid (5.8km) into a walled lane and after a few undulations descend – with some steep sections – into **Kirkby Malham**. Turn left at the T-junction (8.9km), in effect straight ahead, to Malham. Climb then descend into **Malham**.

Malham is attractive in its own right but most visitors, including many students on field trips, come to see the geological features. Malham cove is an 80m sheer curved cliff. Malham beck emerges at the bottom while at the top a prime example of limestone pavement provides microclimates for lime loving plants. Peregrine falcons can be seen nesting near the top.

Gordale Scar is a 100m deep ravine with a couple of waterfalls. Janet's Foss is a small and beautifully set waterfall. Malham Tarn is England's highest lake. The water is trapped by glacial deposits and its distinctly alkaline chemistry is very rare.

Keep left at the main junction in **Malham** (10.9km) towards Arncliffe and Malham Tarn. The climb is steep to begin with but steepens with a few sharp bends to add to the fun. The limestone walls are high but the gates or stiles allow a view of Malham Cove to the right. Gradually the gradient eases and the walls reduce, giving views of the dry valleys, pavement and proud craggy bluffs typical of this limestone area. Turn left at the crossroads (15.1km) towards Langcliffe and Settle. Turn left at the T-junction (15.8km), in effect straight on. Turn right (17.8km) into an unsigned, walled lane which descends gently before a vicious down and up to cross Fornah Gill. Turn right at the T-junction (20.3km) at Sannat Hall Farm to Halton Gill. Ahead lies the bulk of Pen-y-ghent, with its nose-like southern ridge prominent on the left, while to the right the summit of Fountains Fell is hidden by its own slopes.

Climb to **Dale Head** before a gentle descent along the flank of Plover Hill. The gradient increases as Halton Gill and Littondale near. ▶ Cross the River Skirfare. Turn right (30.1km) immediately before **Halton Gill**, cross the small stream and continue down the valley towards Litton and Arncliffe.

There are good long views down the valley.

The floor of the dale is the only level cycling on this stage. To the right you may either see the River Skirfare or just its bed, depending on recent rainfall: this is one of those disappearing rivers. Pass through **Litton** (33.9km). Approaching Arncliffe turn left (37.3km) to and through **Hawkswick**. This narrow lane ambles pleasantly down the dale before descending through open pasture. Turn right at the T-junction (42.7km), cross the river and bend left towards Settle and Grassington. Pass under Kilnsey Crag and through **Kilnsey**.

Kilnsey Crag, a 50m high cliff with a 10m overhang, attracts rock climbers by the score. Grass Wood is ancient woodland which has been designated a SSSI for its woodland flowers. The underlying limestone is present as outcrops, scars, scree and pavement so providing a wide range of habitats.

Turn left (44.1km) to **Conistone** and cross the Wharfe. Bend right (44.7km) in Conistone to Grassington. This road continues all the way to **Grassington**, passing below Grass Wood as it does so.

Enter Grassington, turn right at the T-junction (49.4km) towards Skipton, descend and cross the River Wharfe. Immediately turn left (49.8km) towards Linton. Bend right, climb and turn left at the staggered crossroads to Burnsall. Pass the two turns for Thorpe. Gently descend into **Burnsall** and turn left (55.0km) to Appletreewick.

Burnsall is a charming riverside village set in a glorious location. The stone buildings have a charm and cohesion that is a delight to the eye. The riverside paths are worth walking.

Cross the river, pass the turn for Hebden and pass through **Appletreewick**. Pass the turn for Bolton Abbey (58.2km) and continue towards Pateley Bridge and Skyreholme. The climb is gently at first but steepens considerably as it bends left (58.6km) by the turn for Skyreholme and Parcevall Hall.

Should you wish to visit the 24 acres of recently renovated gardens of **Parcevall Hall**, the largest in the National Park, or Trollers Gill, simply follow the signs.

The steep climb does not last forever. To the right and far below is Trollers Gill, but this is best approached on foot from near Parcevall Hall. Turn right at the T-junction (61.8km) onto the main road to Greenhow Hill and Pateley Bridge. ◄ Climb past **Stump Cross Caverns** and

This section can be busy.

continue up to **Greenhow**. Pass straight through the village, then climb past the limestone quarries on the right. The road is lofty and the views of upper Nidderdale quite extensive.

Coldstones Quarry from Coldstone Cut, Greenhow

Stump Cross Caverns are limestone show caves open to the public. Remains of reindeer, wolves, bison and wolverine have been found.

At over 400m **Greenhow** is one of Yorkshire's highest settlements and it is claimed that that St. Mary's is the highest parish church in England. There is strong evidence that the Romans mined lead here, probably using slave labour. Lead ingots dated AD81 have been found. At Toft Gate there is a signed path to the viewing platform of Coldstone Cut: the platform is an attraction on its own, never mind the views of Nidderdale and beyond.

Pass the Toft Gate Lime Kiln and car park (68.3km). The descent into **Pateley Bridge** is often steep, with some tight corners so take care. Not everyone gets down unscathed. Enter Pateley and at the petrol station is the left turn onto Low Wath Road and the finish point.

PATELEY BRIDGE

Pateley Bridge started as a crossing point of the River Nidd between Ripon and Craven: it was first recorded in the Domesday Survey and granted a market charter in the 14th century. There is a modern public leisure centre with swimming pool and gym. Pateley retains a livestock market, and its agricultural show is held on the third Monday of September.

STAGE 2
Pateley Bridge to Leyburn

Start	Low Wath Road SE 156 654
Finish	Roundabout in the market square SE 111 905
Distance	47.9km/29.9 miles
Total climb	575m
Grade	Medium Hard
Cycling time	2hr 25min
Café stops	How Stean Gorge signed from Lofthouse, Masham (Bordar House Teas) and Leyburn
Parking at start	There are long stay car parks on Nidd Walk, at the showground and on Low Wath Road in the direction of Lofthouse. These car parks do not allow overnight parking. There is free and unrestricted parking in the small car park on Park Road off King Street but it is usually full. There is very limited free and unrestricted on-street parking in town and in nearby Bewerley.

Quiet roads in little visited dales. A pleasant ride in upper Nidderdale, alongside Gouthwaite Reservoir and the River Nidd leads to the leg-burning climb of Trapping Hill into Burn Valley. Rollercoaster roads lead to Masham then continue all the way to Leyburn.

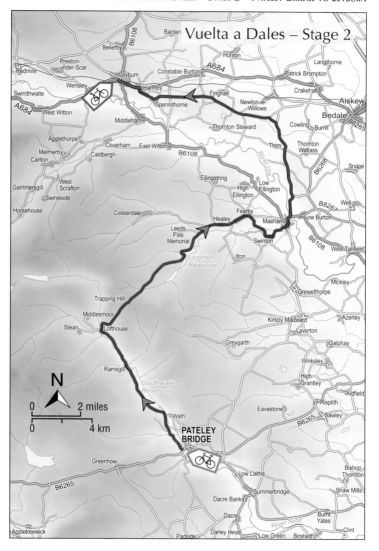

Lofthouse, Nidderdale

Leave Pateley Bridge on Low Wath Road to Ramsgill and Lofthouse. Pass the turns for Heathfield (1.4km) then Wath (2.8km). The road undulates gently but levels alongside **Gouthwaite Reservoir**, built to control the water levels of the River Nidd for the many water powered mills downstream. Pass through **Ramsgill** (7.3km). Approaching Lofthouse there is a small but steep climb

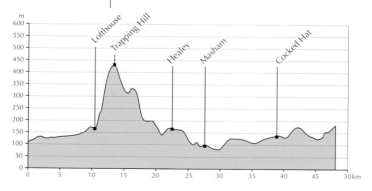

224

followed by descent. Turn right in **Lofthouse** (10.5km) towards Masham.

> Alternatively, to **visit the top end of Nidderdale**, continue straight through Lofthouse and turn right onto the Yorkshire Water access road. The road overlies the bed of the old railway track built for the construction of Scar House and Angram reservoirs. The climb is constant and the going is good. Cyclists are permitted through the top gate up to the second reservoir, Angram.

From Lofthouse the climb up **Trapping Hill** is steep and relentless. The road is narrow with bends and at its steepest is contained by high drystone walls. The top at 429m (13.3km) is marked by a cattle grid. Descend steeply though unenclosed heather moor and grass pasture. The road levels high above Roundhill Reservoir. Descend past Pott Hall before another level section

Approaching Pott Hall, Burn Valley

alongside **Leighton Reservoir**. Descend again, pass the turn for the Leeds Pals Memorial (20.9km), cross the River Burn, pass the Colsterdale and Ellingstring turns and climb to Healey.

> The **Leeds Pals** were the 15th Battalion of the West Yorkshire Regiment. Recruited from the crowded and dirty industrial city of Leeds in September 1914, they were based here for training. For many it would be the best and most carefree time of their lives. In December 1915 they served on the Suez Canal. In the summer of 1916 they moved to France for the Battle of The Somme. Within minutes of Zero Hour (07:30) on the first day of battle there were 528, casualties of whom 248 lay dead. Not one inch of ground was taken. Of the 900 Leeds Pals who fought at the Somme 750 were killed.

Pass through **Healey**, pass the turn for Swinton and Ilton (23.2km), descend and continue through **Fearby**, with its long village green. After a short section of hedged lane turn right at the crossroads (24.4km) to Swinton. Descend, cross the river and climb. Turn left at the T-junction (26.5km) and pass through **Swinton**. Turn left then left again to Masham in front of Swinton Park (27.0km). Descend, cross the river and climb to **Masham**. Turn left at the T-junction (28.3km) and pass through Masham as the road bends right then left.

> **Masham** lays claim to the largest market square in Yorkshire, and the market charter dates back to 1250. It has two breweries, each with its own visitor centre. Importantly for us it has a good range of shops, pubs and cafés. For those who seek a little action the town hosts a Stream Fair and Organ Rally on the third full weekend of July, and in late September there is the sheep fair. Sadly use of the market square as a car park does reduce its attractiveness considerably.

▸ Turn right at the T-junction (29.0km) towards Ripon. Cross the River Ure and turn left (29.4km) towards Thornton Watlass. Pass the turn for Bedale, then pass the turn for Chalcot (32.9km) at Halfpenny House. Continue straight ahead at the crossroads towards **Newton-le-Willows**. Turn left (36.1km) towards Thornton Steward then left again towards Thornton Steward and Spennithorne. Continue on this road, ignoring all turns. Turn left at the T-junction (41.1km) to Spennithorne and continue straight ahead at the two sets of crossroads. Pass the turn for Leyburn (44.4km). Turn right in **Spennithorne** (44.9km) to Harmby and Leyburn. Climb through **Harmby** and turn left at the T-junction (46.2km) to Leyburn. Enter **Leyburn** and pass the turn for Middleham and Ripon. Climb into town and at the far end of the market square is the roundabout that marks the finish point.

The big climbs of the day have now been completed and the remainder of the route is on wide, peaceful, gently undulating roads.

LEYBURN

Located on a shelf well away from the River Ure, Leyburn is the big town in Wensleydale. The River Ure is sometimes referred to as the Yore, and Wensleydale was previously called Yoredale. Although lacking in a colourful history Leyburn is mentioned in the Domesday Book. Its charter was received in 1686 from Charles II and the market is still held on Fridays in the large market place. Leyburn also holds a Dales Food and Drinks Festival over the May Day weekend and an agricultural show in late August. Aided by five main roads that meet here, the town saw rapid growth when the railway opened in 1856. To the east of town on the Shawl, good for views, there are remains of ancient British earthworks.

Approaching the head of Coverdale

STAGE 3
Leyburn to Hawes

Start	Roundabout in the market square SE 111 905
Finish	Market Place SD 871 898
Distance	50.8km/31.8 miles
Total climb	890m
Grade	Long Challenging
Cycling time	2hr 45min
Café stops	Kettlewell, Buckden and Hawes
Parking at start	There is ample free car parking in Leyburn on the market square and nearby, except on Friday which is market day. In addition to day rates, seven-day tickets without overnight restrictions are available in the council's pay and display car park, and these may be used in other Richmondshire District Council and Yorkshire Dales National Park car parks, although some have restrictions.

A day of four contrasting dales. Coverdale is cycled for almost its entire length gaining height all the way. As the dale comes to an end between high gritstone fells so does the first big climb of the day. Wharfedale then Langstrothdale are classic limestone dales which provide excellent cycling. To get to Fleet Moss, the highest road in Yorkshire, the climb is up the challenging dale side. The descent of Sleddale is a joy.

Leave the market square, heading south west from the roundabout towards Wensley and Hawes. Cross the railway, descend through **Wensley** and cross the River Ure. Bend right then turn left (2.6km) to Coverdale and Carlton. Climb and bend right near to the ridge. Pass the turn on the crest (5.0km) and descend through **Agglethorpe** to Melmerby. Continue through **Melmerby** (7.3km) to Carlton and Kettlewell. Turn right at the T-junction (8.0km).

Pass through the strung out village of **Carlton**. The route continues up **Coverdale** in a series of ups

229

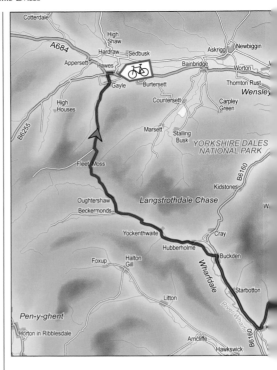

and downs that gradually gain height. Pass through **Gammersgill**, **Horsehouse**, **Braidley** and **Woodale** before crossing onto the south side of the dale (17.6km) by a popular picnic spot. To the head of the dale the climb is relentless and often steep.

The climb peaks at **Little Hunter Stones** (503m) after 21.8km of cycling. ◀ After an initial steep section the road levels before the very steep descent of Park Rash into the pretty valley of Park Gill Beck. Approaching Kettlewell the road bends and steepens. Turn right at the T-junction (25.7km), right again at the crossroads (25.9km) in **Kettlewell**. Turn left at the village stores and turn right at the T-junction (26.1km) with the main road.

The descent is exhilarating.

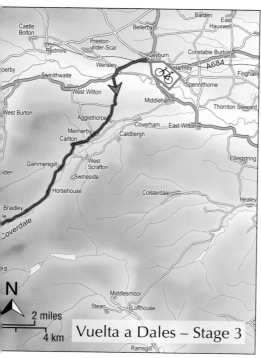

Vuelta a Dales – Stage 3

Pass through **Starbotton**. In **Buckden** turn left (31.8km) to Hubberholme. This part of Wharfedale has steep sides and a wide flat valley floor which continues to Hubberholme, where the dale divides. In **Hubberholme** climb away from the river and pass the George Inn (33.7km). Continue the climb into Langstrothdale, descend through Raisgill and rejoin the river at **Yockenthwaite** (36.2km). Climb gently alongside the river that flows over its pitted limestone bed. After crossing the river climb gently away from it. Bend right by a junction (39.6km) uphill to Hawes. From **Oughtershaw** the climb is unrelenting but with a varying gradient. There are excellent views behind.

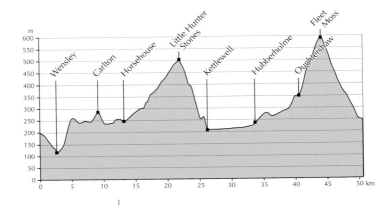

m
600
550
500
450
400
350
300
250
200
150
100
50
0

0   5   10   15   20   25   30   35   40   45   50 km

Wensley · Carlton · Horsehouse · Little Hunter Stones · Kettlewell · Hubberholme · Oughtershaw · Fleet Moss

Wharfedale from Kettlewell

At 589m (44.4km) the road over **Fleet Moss** is the highest road in Yorkshire. Bend left, start to descend then bend right bend by an unsigned road junction (44.9km). Much of the descent down Sleddale has good sight lines,

but there are other vehicles and the road passes through working farms so take care. Enter **Gayle**, bend left over the river and descend into **Hawes**. Turn right at the T-junction with the main road (50.4km) and arrive at the Market Place in the centre of town.

HAWES

Hawes has been a market town since it got its charter in 1699. The market continues every Tuesday. Its name derives from Old Norse and means 'pass between the mountains'. Hawes is a popular spot for visitors and is nearly always busy. There are several museums and the Wensleydale Creamery, with visitor centre, to visit.

STAGE 4
Hawes to Muker

Start	Market Place SD 871 898
Finish	Farmers Arms SD 909 979
Distance	44.4km/27.8 miles
Total climb	535m
Grade	Medium Hard
Cycling time	2hr 15min
Café stops	Askrigg, Bolton Castle, Fremington (The Dales Bike Centre), Reeth, Gunnerside and Muker
Parking at start	There is ample parking in the Yorkshire Dales National Park (YDNP) car park at the Dales Countryside Museum and Richmondshire District Council's (RDC) Gayle Lane car park. In addition to daily parking, seven-day tickets are available in both car parks without overnight restrictions. They may also be used in other RDC and YDNP car parks although some may have restrictions. In addition 24hr and 48hr tickets are available from the YDNP car park. There is limited on-street car parking.

Two completely contrasting dales: Wensleydale – wide, lush and accessible; Swaledale – narrow, hemmed in by fells and timeless. Both, however, so obviously Yorkshire dales. The climb of Greets Moss is challenging and a contrast to the undulating cycling in the dales.

Leave the Market Place heading east. Fork left in compliance with the one way system. Turn left towards Hardraw and Muker. Cross the wide valley floor and cross the Ure. After a short climb turn right (1.6km) towards **Sedbusk** and Askrigg. The undulating road down the dale is on a shelf raised well above the river. Pass all side turns and enjoy the ride. Enter **Askrigg**.

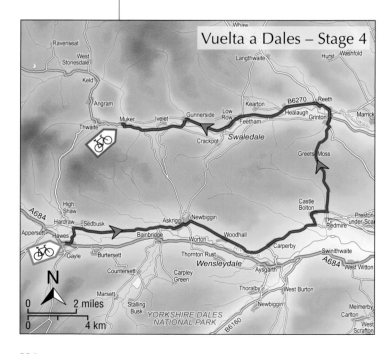

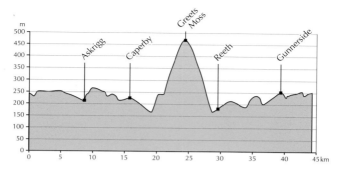

Dominated by the church of Saint Oswald, full of character and set in a sunny location, **Askrigg** has been a market town since 1587. Beside the market cross can be found a steel ring set into the pavement to which bulls were tethered in the days of baiting. The public toilets are in the village hall.

Climb the Main Street and at the top bend right (9.3km) towards Carperby. The climb continues, steep at times. After a bend right continue down the valley with only gentle climbs and descents. Pass through Nappa and **Woodhall**. Pass the turn (15.8km) for Aysgarth and Aysgarth Falls and pass through **Carperby**. Turn left (19.3km) to **Castle Bolton** and climb steeply to the village.

The fortified manor house of **Bolton Castle** dominates Castle Bolton. It has been unoccupied since the Civil War, when the defending Royalists were reduced to eating horseflesh. Its most famous occupant was Mary Queen of Scots, whose unpopularity at home had forced her to abdicate and seek refuge in England. The castle is still owned by the family that built it and is open to the public.

Reeth, Swaledale

Bend right at the castle and pass through the village. Dip into and out of a wooded valley and turn left at the staggered crossroads (21.1km) to Grinton and Reeth. The climb over **Greets Moss** is steep and sustained, and as height is gained heather moor takes over from grass pasture. Bend right after the cattle grid (23.5km) onto open moorland. Cross the watershed at 463m (24.3km) and descend into Swaledale. The descent can be steep with bends. Turn left at the T-junction (27.8km) to Reeth. Descend into **Grinton** and turn left at the T-junction (28.5km), in effect straight ahead. Cross the River Swale, pass through Fremington, cross Arkle Beck and climb into **Reeth**.

Few settlements have a location such as that enjoyed by **Reeth**, spread over a south facing slope and sheltered by hills to the north: sitting above the River Swale, and upstream from its confluence with Arkle Beck, Reeth's aspect is best revealed when approaching from the south.

Originally a Saxon settlement, Reeth was important enough to be included in the Domesday Book. Lead was mined before the Romans came and this continued until just over a century ago. The marks remain to be seen and visited in the surrounding hills. The town got its market charter in 1695.

Pass through Reeth leaving the village green with the Buck Inn (29.9km) on the right towards Gunnerside. Climb steeply out of town. Pass through **Healaugh**. Pass the turn (33.4km) for Askrigg at Low Whita. Climb to and through **Feetham** and **Low Row**. Descend and pass the turn (36.8km) for Crackpot. Continue on the undulated road through woodland to Gunnerside. After the Kings Head in **Gunnerside** bend left (39.5km). Cross the river, bend right and continue up the dale. Pass all turns. Bend right then left to cross Straw Beck and enter Muker.

Hay Meadows, Muker, Swaledale

MUKER

Set in an idyllic location Muker is a jewel in Yorkshire's crown, a village in harmony with its landscape. It is here that Swaledale loses its road for some 5km, allowing walkers a rare opportunity to experience the Dale as it may have appeared to its Bronze Age or Viking visitors. A short walk across the hay meadows to the river is all that is required. So get on with it. Those staying at the campsite can enjoy a walk across the fields past field barns to the village, continue to the Swale and return by the Farmers Arms.

STAGE 5
Muker to Sedbergh

Start	Farmers Arms SD 909 979
Finish	A684 outside the Duo Café SD 657 921
Distance	44.5km/27.8 miles
Total climb	595m
Grade	Medium Hard
Cycling time	2hr 20min
Café stops	Thwaite (Kearton Country Hotel) and Sedbergh
Parking at start	In addition to day rates Richmondshire District Council's (RDC) pay-and-display car park issues seven-day tickets without overnight restrictions. They may also be used in other RDC and Yorkshire Dales National Park car parks, although some may have restrictions. There is very limited on-street car parking in Muker but some roadside parking just west of the village.

Swaledale retains its narrowness and beauty to the very end, where Birkdale takes over. Surrounded by distant hills and devoid of much human presence, it can be very bleak. An extended descent ends with a short ride alongside the River Eden. As Sedbergh nears the rounded, grass covered Howgill Fells rise higher until they dominate the town.

Leave Muker heading west towards Keld and Kirkby Stephen. Pass Usha Gap campsite, cross the beck and climb. Pass the turn for Hawes, descend and pass through **Thwaite**. Continue through **Angram** to **Keld** on a hilly road well above the dale bottom. Pass the 'Keld only' turns (5.0km).

Swaledale from Thwaite

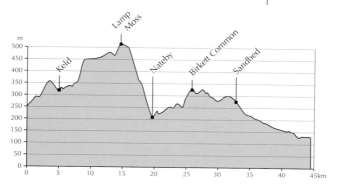

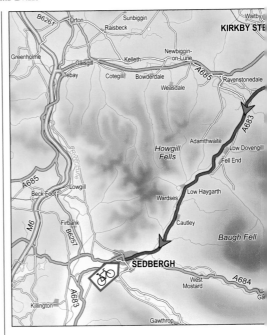

Keld was once a major lead mining centre and is ideally placed for visits to the waterfalls of upper Swaledale. Downstream are Catrake and Kidston Forces and upstream is Wain Wath Force, which can be seen from the route. Expect a lot of walkers, as both the Pennine Way and Coast to Coast walks cross here.

Descend and pass the turn for **West Stonesdale** (5.9km). A level section is accompanied by waterfalls and crags. Cross the beck and climb steeply. Pass the turn for Ravenseat (8.9km), where the gradient eases. The climb soon resumes along the side of **Birkdale** on a mostly unenclosed road. Signs of human habitation soon disappear and heather moorland takes over.

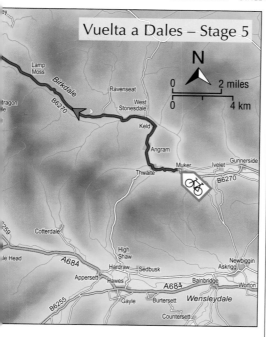

Vuelta a Dales – Stage 5

The road peaks at 519m at **Lamp Moss** (14.8km).
Enter Cumbria and after a short level section descend,
steeply at times, to Nateby. Here are good views of
Mallerstang Common and Edge. Turn left at the T-junction
(19.7km) in **Nateby** by the Black Bull Inn towards Hawes.
Gently climb Mallerstang Common on a road that sometimes runs beside the River Eden. Turn right (24.2km) into
an unsigned lane at **Pendragon Castle**.

> Legend has it that **Pendragon Castle** was built by
> King Arthur's father Uther Pendragon. It is actually
> 12th century.

Cross the river and climb via a series of bends to
the unenclosed **Birkett Common**. Descend and turn left

Cautley Crag and Cautley Spout, Howgill Fells

A walk to them is always worth the effort. ◀

at the T-junction (27.5km). The route continues directly to Sedbergh so all turns can be ignored. Pass Sandbed (32.8km), where the landscape changes from limestone to the slates and shales of the Howgill Fells. The descent is undulating and as height is lost the Howgills loom larger and larger. Cross the River Rawthey (35.2km) into Rawtheydale. Cautley Crag and Cautley Spout (England's highest waterfall) reveal themselves in a deep dale on the right. ◀

Pass through **Cautley** and continue on to Sedbergh. Enter **Sedbergh**, pass the turn for Garsdale and Hawes (43.8km), turn right at the roundabout (44.4km) and at the left bend is the finish point.

SEDBERGH

Sedbergh is the most westerly market town in the National Park. It sits tucked into the foot of the Howgill Fells, while its own feet are washed by the River Rawthey. The Howgills are composed largely of slate and this dark grey rock gives the local buildings their character. Many buildings in the area, including Dentdale, have been whitewashed. Sedbergh's wealth was based on the wool industry but this has gone and the town depends on agriculture, tourism, light industry and the independent schools. Recently there has been a move to develop the town into the northern Hay-on-Wye, hence the number of bookshops.

STAGE 6
Sedbergh to Settle

Start	On A684 outside the Duo Café SD 657 921
Finish	Whitefriars Court car park SD 819 638
Distance	45.9km/28.7 miles
Total climb	715m
Grade	Medium Challenging
Cycling time	2hr 30min
Café stops	Dent, Ingleton and Settle
Parking at start	There are two car parks close to the centre of Sedbergh, good for day visits only. The Joss Lane car park is used for the weekly Wednesday market. There is free and unrestricted on-street parking away from the town centre.

The grey slate architecture of Dentdale leads back to classic karst landscape via the challenging climb over White Stone Moss into Kingsdale. Kingsdale, wide and full of crags and potholes (of the limestone, rather than tarmac, variety), is a cycling treat. From Ingleton the route climbs along the southern flank of Ingleborough before heading back through stunning limestone country into Ribblesdale and back to Settle.

Leave Sedbergh heading south on Finkle Street in the direction of Dent. Continue straight ahead at the roundabout towards Dent. Pass the turn for Kendal. Continue downhill and cross the river. Bend right and climb gently. Pass the turn for Sedbergh Golf Club (1.8km) and then pass the turn for Holme Open Farm (3.1km). Continue up the dale, bend right to cross the River Dee, pass the turn for Gawthrop (7.8km) and enter **Dent**.

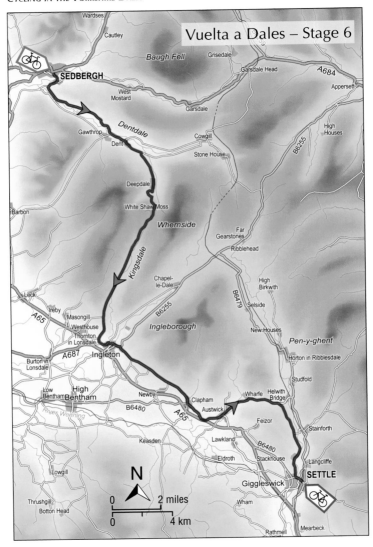

*Kingsdale from
Kingsdale Head*

Dentdale is beautiful from top to bottom. The lower dale is largely slate, the upper limestone. This is reflected in the buildings and walls, where they exist, for Dentdale has many hedges. The popular village of Dent is very pretty, with its whitewashed cottages and cobbled streets. Late June sees a music and beer festival. Dent railway station near Cowgill at 350m is the highest on the network in England.

Turn right (8.9km) by the George and Dragon to Deepdale and Ingleton. Leave Dent, climbing gently. Turn right (10.1km) to Ingleton and Clapham. The climb up **Deepdale** is often steep, particularly at its head, with only the scenery and the odd waterfall to distract. Towards the top of the climb the road is gated. The watershed of **White Shaw Moss** is at 473m (14.8km). Descend to and pass Kingsdale Head (17.8km), where the gradient eases greatly, for the final gate of the day. Kingsdale is full of nothing but grand scenery, limestone scars, potholers and the occasional farm.

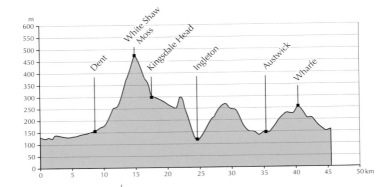

Climb out of the dale, descend, pass the turn with the panorama (22.9km) and enter **Thornton in Lonsdale**. Turn left at the T-junction (24.4km) opposite the Marton Arms Hotel to Ingleton. Bend left by a junction (24.6km) then turn left at the T-junction (24.8km) towards Clapham. Descend into **Ingleton**, pass under the viaduct, pass the waterfalls walk entrance and cross the two rivers.

Ingleton is set in a steep sided valley, where the rivers Doe and Twiss join to become the Greta. The local limestone is riddled with holes. It has a seasonal open air heated swimming pool for a mid-ride dip. The big draw, however, is the Ingleton Waterfalls Trail, an 8km walk through ancient woodland passing many waterfalls and geological features.

Bend left (25.5km) and climb to the village centre. Turn left at the T-junction, in compliance with the one way system. Pass through the town centre. The road bends right and climbs. Turn left and uphill at the T-junction (26.0km) towards Hawes then turn right (26.3km) to Clapham. ◀ The climb is gradual before a steep descent into **Clapham**. Pass the turn for the Yorkshire Cycle Way (32.0km), then turn left at the T-junction (32.4km). Cross

This wide road has views south to the Forest of Bowland.

Austwick

the river then bend sharp right then left to get round the New Inn. At the A65 turn left (33.9km) towards Skipton using either the main road or the parallel bridleway. The road is usually very busy and carries a lot of freight. Turn left (34.4km) to Austwick.

In **Austwick** turn left at the pillar (35.5km) towards Horton. The walled road narrows and climbs though a craggy and broken limestone landscape. Turn right at the crossroads (39.8km) and climb gently. Pass straight through Little Stainforth (42.0km) and Stackhouse. Enter **Giggleswick** and turn left at the T-junction (45.2km) to Settle. Cross the river, pass the turn for Langcliffe and enter **Settle**. Pass under the viaduct to arrive at the Whitefriars Court car park.

APPENDIX A

Route summary table

No	Grade	Start	Title	Loop/Linear	Distance (km/miles)	Climb (m)	Page
1	Long Hard	Pateley Bridge	Nidderdale, Washburn and Wharfedale	Loop	65.9/41.2	835	38
2	Medium Hard	Pateley Bridge	Brimham Moor, Fountains Abbey and Studley Royal	Loop	44.5/27.8	575	47
3	Long Hard	Pateley Bridge	Masham and Burn Valley	Loop	53.9/33.7	715	52
4	Medium Moderate	Grassington	Round Barden	Loop	41.3/25.8	455	59
5	Long Hard	Grassington	Malhamdale and High Limestone Country	Loop	49.4/30.9	710	65
6	Medium Challenging	Grassington	Malhamdale by way of Bordley	Loop	32.6/20.4	605	71
7	Long Moderate	Grassington	Malhamdale, Silverdale and Littondale	Loop	71.8/44.9	760	75
8	Medium Challenging	Ingleton	Dentdale and round Whernside	Loop	44.9/28.1	730	84
9	Medium Moderate	Ingleton	Ribblesdale and round Ingleborough	Loop	37.9/23.7	405	90
10	Long Challenging	Settle	Dale and Tarn	Loop	49.1/30.7	855	96
11	Short Challenging	Settle	Langcliffe Scar and Malham	Loop	25.7/16.1	545	103
12	Medium Hard	Reeth	Tan Hill	Loop	45.0/28.1	580	107
13	Long Hard	Reeth	Wensleydale, Mallerstang and Tan Hill	Loop	92.2/57.6; via Birkdale and Swaledale: 87.2/54.5	1250; via Birkdale and Swaledale: 1100	111

APPENDIX A – ROUTE SUMMARY TABLE

No	Grade	Start	Title	Loop/Linear	Distance (km/miles)	Climb (m)	Page
14	Long Hard/Medium Hard	Reeth	Richmond	Loop	52.4/32.8; via Marske: 35.7/22.3	730; via Marske: 535	125
15	Medium Moderate	Sedbergh	Lune Valley and Barbondale	Loop	44.1/27.6	485	134
16	Medium Moderate/Long Moderate	Sedbergh	Circuit of the Howgill Fells/via Mallerstang	Loop	45.1/28.2; via Mallerstang: 62.9/39.3	490; via Mallerstang: 625	140
17	Short Hard	Sedbergh	Barbondale and Holme Open Farm	Loop	29.7/18.6	385	149
18	Long Challenging	Hawes	The Big Cheese	Loop	62.5/39.1	1220	154
19	Short Challenging	Hawes	Semerwater	Loop	19.3/12.1	350	159
20	Long Challenging	Hawes	Coverdale and Langstrothdale Chase	Loop	70.7/44.2; via Bishopdale: 50.9/31.8	1175; via Bishopdale: 910	162
21	Medium Challenging	Leyburn	Swaledale and The Fleak	Loop	44.8/28	765	175
22	Short Hard	Leyburn	Aysgarth Falls	Loop	26.9/16.8	360	181
23	Short Moderate	Leyburn	Jervaulx Abbey and Middleham	Loop	23.9/14.9	205	185
Tour de France 2014							
24	Long Moderate	Leeds	Tour de France 2014 Stage 1: Leeds to Harrogate	Linear/Loop	205.8/128.6 or 201.4/125.9	2125 or 2030	190
La Vuelta a Dales							
Stage 1	Long Hard	Settle	Pateley Bridge	Linear	71.2/44.5	1030	215
Stage 2	Medium Hard	Pateley Bridge	Leyburn	Linear	47.9/29.9	575	222
Stage 3	Long Challenging	Leyburn	Hawes	Linear	50.8/31.8	890	229
Stage 4	Medium Hard	Hawes	Muker	Linear	44.4/27.8	535	233
Stage 5	Medium Hard	Muker	Sedbergh	Linear	44.5/27.8	595	238
Stage 6	Medium Challenging	Sedbergh	Settle	Linear	45.9/28.7	715	243

249

APPENDIX B
Useful contacts

*M=mountain bike, H=hybrid, C=Child seat/tag-along, R=road cycle, T=tandem

Cycle shops and cycle hire

Cycle sales and repairs				
		Website	**Telephone**	**Bike type***
Bedale	Blaze A Trail		01677 427831	
Catterick Garrison	Bank Cycles	www.bankcycles.co.uk	01748 836143	MHR
Fremington	Dales Bike Centre	www.dalesbikecentre.co.uk	01748 884908	M
Gargrave	JD Tandems	www.tandems.co.uk	01756 748400	T
Harrogate	Boneshakers	www.boneshakerscycles.co.uk	01423 709453	MHR
Harrogate	Halfords	www.halfords.com	01423 887102	MHR
Harrogate	Spa Cycles	www.spacycles.co.uk	01423 887003	MHR
Ilkley	J D Cycles	www.jdcycles.co.uk	01943 816101	MHR
Ingleton	Escape Bikes	www.escapebikeshop.com	015242 41226	MHR
Keighley	Aire Valley Cycles	www.airevalleycycles.com	01535 280804	MHR
Keighley	Halfords	www.halfords.com	01535 600479	MHR
Kendal	Askew Cycles	www.askewcycles.com	01539 728057	MHR
Kendal	Evans Cycles	www.evanscycles.com	01539 740087	MHR
Kendal	Halfords	www.halfords.com	01539 735001	MHR
Kendal	Wheelbase	www.wheelbase.co.uk	01539 821443	MHR
Leeds	Edinburgh Bicycle Co-operative	www.edinburghbicycle.com	0113 268 7463	MHR
Leeds	Evans Cycles	www.evanscycles.com	0113 246 9132	MHR
Leeds	Halfords	www.halfords.com	0113 278 0144	MHR
Leyburn	Leyburn Bike	www.leyburnbikes.co.uk	01969 623565	M
Northallerton	Cowley Cycles	www.cowleycycles.co.uk	01609 776656	MHR
Northallerton	Halfords	www.halfords.com	01609 767750	MHR
Otley	Chevin Cycles	www.chevincycles.com	01943 462773	MHR
Richmond	Arthur Caygill	www.arthurcaygillcycles.co.uk	01748 906059	MHR
Ripon	Moonglu Cycles	www.moonglu.com	01765 601106	MHR
Settle	3 Peaks Cycles	www.3peakscycles.com	01729 824232	MHR
Skipton	Dave Ferguson	www.daveferguson.com	01756 795367	MHR

Cycle sales and repairs

		Website	Telephone	Bike type*
Skipton	The Bicycle Shop	wwwbicycleshop.co.uk	01756 794386	MHR
Summerbridge	Stif Cycles	www.stif.co.uk	01423 780738	MHR

Cycle hire

		Website	Telephone	Bike type*
Aysgarth	Aysgarth Bike Hire	www.aysgarthbikehire.co.uk	01969 663534	M
Fremington	Dales Bike Centre	www.dalesbikecentre.co.uk	01748 884908	MHC
Kendal	Wheelbase	www.wheelbase.co.uk	01539 821443	MC
Lancashire	Cycle Adventure	www.cycle-adventure.co.uk	07518 373 007	MC
Ravenstonedale	Stonetrail	www.stonetrailholidays.com	015396 23444	M
Settle	Off The Rails	www.offtherails.org.uk	01729 824419	HC
Skipton	Dave Ferguson	www.davefergusoncycles.com	01756 795367	

General cycle repairs

		Website	Telephone
Catterick	Bikanic Mobile Cycle Repairs		07801 053930
Kirkby Lonsdale	Dales Bike Doctor	www.dalesbikedoctor.co.uk	015242 73195
Skipton	Riders Cycle	www.riderscyclescentre.com	01756 796844

National Park and Tourist Information Centres

	Website	Telephone
Aysgarth	National Park Visitor Centre	01969 662910
Grassington	National Park Visitor Centre	01756 751690
Harrogate	Tourist Information Centre	0845 389 3223
Hawes	Tourist Information Office	01969 666210
Horton in Ribblesdale	Tourist Information Centre	01729 860333
Ingleton	Tourist Information Centre	015242 41049
Kirkby Stephen	Tourist Information Centre	01768 371199
Leeds	Tourist Information Centre	0113 242 5242
Leyburn	Tourist Information Office	01969 622317

National Park and Tourist Information Centres		
	Website	**Telephone**
Malham	National Park Visitor Centre	01729 833200
Pateley Bridge	Tourist Information Centre	0845 389 0178
Reeth	Tourist Information Centre	01748 884059
Richmond	Tourist Information Centre	01748 828742
Ripon	Tourist Information Centre	0845 389 0178
Sedbergh	Tourist Information Office	015396 20125
Settle	Tourist Information Centre	01729 825192
Skipton	Tourist Information Centre	01756 792809

Car hire		
	Website	**Telephone**
Avis	www.avis.co.uk	08445 818181
Budget	www.budget.co.uk	08445 443455
Europcar	www.europcar.co.uk	0845 758 5375
Hertz	www.hertz.co.uk	0843 309 3099
Holiday Autos	www.holidayautos.co.uk	0800 093 3111

APPENDIX C
Campsites along the Vuelta a Dales

Some campsites are open all year but many are seasonal. There may be restrictions as to group size or mix and others may require a minimum stay during popular periods such as Bank Holiday weekends. Inclusion is not an endorsement.

Stage 1
Settle
Langcliffe Caravan Park,
Langcliffe
Tel 01729 822387

Knight Stainforth Hall
Caravan and Camping Park,
Little Stainforth
Tel 01729 822200

Malham
Riverside Campsite,
Malham Cove,
Town Head Farm
Tel 01729 830287

Gordale Scar Camp Site,
Gordale Farm
Tel 01729 830333

National Trust,
Malham Tarn,
Waterhouses
Tel 01729 830416

Arncliffe
Hawkswick Cote Caravan Park
Tel 01756 770226

Threshfield
Wood Nook Caravan Park,
Skirethorns
Tel 01756 752412

Appletreewick
Masons Camp Site,
Ainhams House
Tel 01756 720275

Howarth Farm Caravan Park,
Skyreholme
Tel 01756 720226

Pateley Bridge
Riverside Caravan Park,
Low Wath Road
Tel 01423 711383

Heathfield Caravan Park,
Ramsgill Road
Tel 01423 711652

Low Wood Caravan Park,
Spring House,
Heathfield
Tel 01423 711433

Westfield Farm,
Heathfield
Tel 01423 711880

Stage 2
Lofthouse
Studfold Caravan and Camping Park
Tel 01423 755084

How Stean Gorge
Tel 01423 755666

Masham
Black Swan Country Park,
Fearby
Tel 01765 689477

Old Station Holiday Park,
Low Burton
Tel 01765 689569

Leyburn
Craken House Caravan Site,
Middleham Road
Tel 01969 622204

Pheasant Inn and Caravan Park,
Harmby
Tel 01969 622223

Yorkshire Dales Country Park,
Harmby
Tel 08700 444444

Stage 3

Buckden
Heber Farm Certificated Site
Tel 01756 760304

Hawes
Bainbridge Ings
Tel 01969 667354

The Green Dragon Inn Campsite,
Hardraw
Tel 01969 667392

Old Hall Cottage Camping Site,
The Cart House
Tel 01969 667691

Shaw Ghyll Farm,
Simonstone
Tel 01969 667359

Stage 4

Redmire
Swan Farm
Tel 01969 622331

Grinton
The Bridge Inn
Tel 01748 884224

Reeth
Orchard Caravan and Camping Park,
Cricket Field
Tel 01748 884475

Low Row
Scabba Wath Campsite,
Low Whita Farm
Tel 01748 884601

Muker
Usha Gap Campsite
Tel 01748 886214

Stage 5

Keld
Rukins Campsite Park Lodge
Tel 01748 886274

Park House Camping
and Keld Bunkhouse
Tel 01748 886549

Hoggarths Farm Campsite
Tel 01748 886335

Kirkby Stephen
Pennine View Caravan Park,
Station Road
Tel 01768 371717

Ravenstonedale
Bowber Head Camping Site
Tel 01539 623254

Low Greenside Farm,
Greenside Lane
Tel 015396 23217

Sedbergh
Cross Hall Camp Site,
Cautley
Tel 01539 620668

Lincolns Inn Camp Site,
Firbank
Tel 01539 620567

Holme Open Farm
Tel 015396 20654

Stage 6

Dent
Mill Beck Farm Camp Site,
Mill Beck Farm
Tel 01539 625424

High Laning Camping
and Caravan Park
Tel 015396 25239

Conder Farm Campsite,
Deepdale Road
Tel 015396 25277

Ingleton
Moorgarth Farm Campsite,
New Road
Tel 01524 241428

Austwick
Dalesbridge
Tel 01524 251021

Silloth House,
Wharfe
Tel 07854 368832

Woodend Campsite
Tel 015242 51296

Helwith Bridge
Helwith Bridge Campsite
Tel 01729 860422

APPENDIX D
Cycles on public transport

Each rail company in Britain has its own policy on the carriage of cycles on its trains. Train staff are often friendly and flexible in interpreting company policies but this should not be relied on. Those with tandems, tricycles, trailers and powered cycles can almost write off carriage by train.

Maintenance of railway lines is often carried out at weekends and during public holidays. The replacement service is usually a bus on which only packed folding cycles could be expected to be carried. For general rail enquiries contact National Rail Enquiries; telephone 08457 484950, textphone service 0845 605 0600 or www.nationalrail.co.uk.

Buses within the Dales and those from further afield do not carry cycles except packed folding cycles subject to space being available.

Northern Rail
Northern Rail claims a strong commitment to promote cycling as a sustainable and healthy means of transport that complements its train services. In reality this support to cycling is leaving your cycle at the station then taking a train.

Up to two cycles can be carried on any one train at the conductor's discretion. There is no charge but spaces cannot be reserved which limits the appeal for those who need to plan their visit. Cycle spaces should be clearly marked and are available on a first come first served basis. Note that tandems, tricycles, trailers and power assisted cycles are not allowed.

www.northernrail.org
Tel 0845 600 8008

Services out of Leeds
- Ilkley (Route 1) with a stop at Ben Rhydding (Route 1)
- Carlisle via the Settle–Carlisle Railway with stops at Settle (Routes 10, 11 and VaD Stage 1), Horton in Ribblesdale (Route 9), Ribblehead (Routes 8 and 9), Dent (Routes 8 and 18), Garsdale (Routes 13, 16 Option and 18), Kirkby Stephen (Routes 13 and VaD Stage 5)
- Carnforth with stops at Giggleswick (Route 10) and Clapham (Routes 9 and VaD Stage 6)

Wensleydale Railway
The Wensleydale Railway exists because the local community wanted to re-open the former line and were prepared to do the work. It opened in 2003 and currently runs trains between Leeming Bar and Redmire with stops at Bedale, Finghall (Route 23), Leyburn

(Routes 21, 22 and VaD Stage 2) and Redmire (Routes 21, 22, 23 and VaD Stage 4). There are plans to extend east to Northallerton and west to Garsdale.

Cycles are conveyed free when space is available. More than six cycles must be booked in advance.

www.wensleydalerailway.com
Tel 08454 50 54 74
or for group booking 01677 42580

East Coast

East Coast run trains between London Kings Cross, Leeds, York, Northallerton, Edinburgh and Aberdeen. Leeds station has connections with Northern Rail. The market town of Northallerton is on the edge of the Dales and an easy nine kilometre ride from the Wensleydale Railway at Leeming Bar. There is a Link Route from Northallerton to Leyburn via Leeming Bar at the beginning of the Leyburn section, before Route 21.

Five cycles can be carried on each train for which there is no charge but a reservation is required. This can be done when buying your ticket. Reservations can be made either on line, at a rail travel centre or at an East Coast station 24 hours before travel. Folded Brompton type cycles can be carried as normal luggage without restriction. Note that tandems, tricycles, trailers and power assisted cycles are not allowed.

www.eastcoast.co.uk
Tel 08457 225 111

First Transpennine Express

Transpennine Express run trains from Manchester across the Pennines before turning north. Services connect Manchester Airport with Leeds, York and Northallerton. The market town of Northallerton is on the edge of the Dales and an easy nine kilometre ride from the Wensleydale Railway at Leeming Bar. There is a Link Route from Northallerton to Leyburn via Leeming Bar at the beginning of the Leyburn section, before Route 21.

Up to two cycles can be reserved in advance at no charge otherwise its first come first served. Folded Brompton type cycles can be carried as normal luggage without restriction. Note that tandems, tricycles, trailers and power assisted cycles are not allowed.

www.tpexpress.co.uk
Tel 0845 600 1674

Cross Country Trains

Cross Country Trains run trains from England's midlands, south-west and south-centre to Leeds, York and Northallerton. These include trains from Stanstead, Birmingham and Southampton airports. The market town of Northallerton is on the edge of the Dales and an easy nine kilometre ride from the Wensleydale Railway at Leeming Bar. There is a Link Route from Northallerton to Leyburn via Leeming Bar at the beginning of the Leyburn section, before Route 21.

Up to two cycles can be reserved in advance at no charge otherwise its first come first served. Folded Brompton type cycles can be carried as normal luggage without restriction. Note that tandems, tricycles, trailers and power assisted cycles are not allowed.

www.crosscountrytrains.co.uk
Tel 0844 811 0124

Grand Central
Grand Central run trains from London Kings Cross to Sunderland via York and Northallerton. The market town of Northallerton is on the edge of the Dales and an easy nine kilometre ride from the Wensleydale Railway at Leeming Bar. There is a Link Route from Northallerton to Leyburn via Leeming Bar at the beginning of the Leyburn section, before Route 21.

Cyclists are able to use all Central trains. Reservation is not compulsory but large groups should call in advance to check the capacity of space on a particular train. Tandemists and tricyclists are also advised to check.

www.grandcentralrail.co.uk
Tel 0845 603 4852

APPENDIX E
Basic bike maintenance

Tools and spares

A well maintained cycle should give little trouble. However, do expect to do the odd adjustment and occasional repair. Appendix A lists cycle shops that should be able to help with any serious repairs. The following is a list of tools that the author would normally carry on both single and multi-day rides. They should be sufficient to adjust, remove and tighten brakes, pedals and pannier racks. Groups may wish to share items to minimise weight:

- Puncture repair kit
- Spare inner tube - of the size and type fitted to the cycle
- Pump that will inflate to the recommended tyre pressure
- Tyre levers
- Multi-tool complete with flat and cross point screw drivers, Allen-keys (typically 4, 5, 6 and 7mm)
- Should the wheels not have quick-release mechanisms a multi-head spanner will be required
- Oil which can be left at base

Daily check

Before making a trip to the Dales it is recommended that cycles are checked, adjusted or repaired either by their owners or the local cycle shop. Those confident in their mechanical skills but not that experienced with cycle maintenance should find *The Bike Book* published by Haynes a reliable manual.

A pre-ride safety check is always recommended. An easy system to use is the M check which examines the cycle following an M shaped path.

1. Start at the front wheel hub: Check that the quick-release or axel bolts hold the wheel securely in place.

2. Move up the front fork to the brake: Apply the front brake looking for an even application of the pads to the wheel rims without excessive movement of the brake lever. There should be plenty of the brake pads remaining. Lift the front of the cycle and check that the wheel spins freely without any buckles. Grip the rim check for side to side play which would indicate worn bearings in the hub. Check the tyre for wear or damage and remove any embedded foreign objects such as flint chips or pieces of glass. Check the tyres are inflated to the manufacturers' recommended pressures.

3. Move up to the handlebars: With the brake applied and both hands on the handlebars rock the cycle back and forth checking for play in the steering tube. You don't want any. The handlebars should

be at right angles to the wheel. Check the brake and gear levers work. Visually inspect the cables and cable outers for damage, rust or fraying.

4   Move down the down tube to the bottom bracket: Check the frame tube and any cables on the way. Hold both pedal cranks and push both down at the same time then side to side checking for any play. Play or clunking shouldn't be there. Check that the pedals spin freely and without play. Check the chain for free movement and lubrication by turning the pedals backwards for a few revolutions. The chain should purr.

5   Move up the seat tube: Check that the seat post is secure. Check that the saddle is secure and correctly aligned. This is best done by looking from behind.

6   Move down to the rear brake and perform the same checks on the brake, tyre and rim as for the front brake. Visually check any cables and outers that run along the top tube.

7   Move down to the rear hub: Check that the quick-release or axel bolts hold the wheel securely in place.

8   Perform the same checks on the rear wheel and tyre as the front one.

Check that accessories such as lights, bottle cages etc work and are tightly secured as you pass.

Take a short ride to check out the gear changing and indexing.

Appendix B lists cycle shops that should be able to help with repairs or maintenance should you need help.

Punctures

Punctures are never welcome and nor convenient. Fortunately there are strategies to reduce the chance of them happening.

There are a number of airless tyres on the market which come pre-filled with foam. They cannot puncture. However, they generally give less cushioning than a pneumatic tyre, have a greater rolling resistance and so are more suited to urban roads.

Some tyres are more puncture resistant than others. They have a dense belt of Kevlar or similar threads under the tread. Tyres from Continental have proven particularly good in this aspect. Their Grand Prix 4000S is well suited for racing cycles and the GatorSkin for touring cycles.

Keep tyres inflated to the manufacturers recommended pressure and check for and remove embedded splinters, glass and flints before a ride. Check for thorns after passing freshly clipped hedges. Seek out and inspect deep cuts. Badly worn tyres are a puncture magnet.

It is possible to buy inner-tubes that contain a self sealing liquid. The liquid fills the puncture and solidifies so sealing the hole. There may be a small loss of air pressure and the liquid slows wheel rotation. The same liquid can be squeezed into an inner-tube although there may be problems if you have Presta valves without removable cores. Look out for the trade name Slime.

For a quick roadside repair Geax supply Pitstop, a combined latex sealant and inflator. Not cheap but useful in bad weather when changing an inner-tube really is the last thing you want to do.

Changing an inner-tube

Those not experienced at changing tubes are advised to practice in the peace and quiet of their own homes rather than on the roadside. It is invariably easier to work on the wheel with it removed from the frame. Swapping out the punctured inner tube for a spare and repairing the hole later will save time.

Remove the wheel from the cycle. This usually requires releasing the brake to allow refitting later.

Inspect the tyre for evidence of the puncture point. Note its position relative to the valve stem. Remove any embedded objects.

Remove the valve dust cap and locking ring. With Presta valves loosen the knurled valve centre and release any remaining air. With Schrader valves simply press the central pin.

Run a tyre lever between the rim and the tyre to release the whole tyre. Do both sides.

Starting opposite the valve, insert a tyre lever, hook the inner rim of the tyre and work it over the rim of the wheel. Take care not to catch the inner tube. Pushing the valve stem partially into the wheel will often make this easier. Working towards the valve use a second tyre lever to lever the remaining tyre over the rim. Only one side of the tyre needs removing.

Starting opposite the valve gently pull the inner-tube from the tyre. With the inner-tube removed inspect the tyre for the puncture hole or holes and remove anything embedded. This inspection should include the inside if the tyre. Run your thumb round the inside of the tyre feeling for any foreign objects; be gentle as they may be sharp. Use a hard flat tool to push back out well embedded objects such as thorns.

Check that the rim tape is centrally located.

Fit the repaired or replacement tube back inside the tyre locating the valve stem first. Pump a small amount of air in to give it some shape.

Fit the tyre back onto the rim starting at the valve. Reverse the removal process and make sure that the valve stem is at right angles to the rim. Take care not to pinch the inner tube. When the tyre is in place inflate a little more. Work round the wheel and on both side squeeze the tyre away from the wheel rim to make sure that the inner-tube is correctly located and not trapped between tyre and wheel.

Inflate the tyre and check that the tyre is correctly seated on the rim. Refit any locking ring and dust cap. Refit the wheel to the cycle and reset the bakes. Perform the daily check for this part of the cycle.

Repair of a punctured inner tube

Inflate the tube to locate the puncture. Listen carefully for the hiss of escaping air or immerse in water and look for bubbles. Some slow punctures are caused by a faulty valve or by the valve stem separating from the tube. These faults are usually not repairable. There could be more than one puncture.

Gently roughen the area around the hole using the emery or glass paper provided. The area should be larger than the patch being fitted.

Apply a small dab of glue and spread over an area larger than the patch. Allow to dry so that it is on the dry side of tacky.

Peel the patch from the foil backing and locate centrally over the puncture. Press firmly onto the puncture site working outwards to squeeze out any trapped air and to ensure the edges are sealed. Allow the repair to cure for a few minutes.

Test the repair by partially inflating the tube. Inspect for leaks and check that pressure is being held.

NOTES

NOTES

NOTES

NOTES

LISTING OF CICERONE GUIDES

BRITISH ISLES CHALLENGES, COLLECTIONS AND ACTIVITIES
The End to End Trail
The Mountains of England and Wales: 1&2
The National Trails
The Relative Hills of Britain
The Ridges of England, Wales and Ireland
The UK Trailwalker's Handbook
The UK's County Tops
Three Peaks, Ten Tors

UK CYCLING
Border Country Cycle Routes
Cycling in the Cotswolds
Cycling in the Hebrides
Cycling in the Peak District
Cycling in the Yorkshire Dales
Cycling the Pennine Bridleway
Mountain Biking in the Lake District
Mountain Biking in the Yorkshire Dales
Mountain Biking on the North Downs
Mountain Biking on the South Downs
The C2C Cycle Route
The End to End Cycle Route
The Lancashire Cycleway

SCOTLAND
Backpacker's Britain
    Central and Southern Scottish Highlands
    Northern Scotland
Ben Nevis and Glen Coe
Great Mountain Days in Scotland
Not the West Highland Way
Scotland's Best Small Mountains
Scotland's Far West
Scotland's Mountain Ridges
Scrambles in Lochaber
The Ayrshire and Arran Coastal Paths
The Border Country
The Cape Wrath Trail
The Great Glen Way
The Isle of Mull
The Isle of Skye
The Pentland Hills

The Scottish Glens 2 – The Atholl Glens
The Southern Upland Way
The Speyside Way
The West Highland Way
Walking Highland Perthshire
Walking in Scotland's Far North
Walking in the Angus Glens
Walking in the Cairngorms
Walking in the Ochils, Campsie Fells and Lomond Hills
Walking in Torridon
Walking Loch Lomond and the Trossachs
Walking on Harris and Lewis
Walking on Jura, Islay and Colonsay
Walking on Rum and the Small Isles
Walking on the Isle of Arran
Walking on the Orkney and Shetland Isles
Walking on Uist and Barra
Walking the Corbetts
    1 South of the Great Glen
    2 North of the Great Glen
Walking the Galloway Hills
Walking the Lowther Hills
Walking the Munros
    1 Southern, Central and Western Highlands
    2 Northern Highlands and the Cairngorms
Winter Climbs Ben Nevis and Glen Coe
Winter Climbs in the Cairngorms
World Mountain Ranges: Scotland

NORTHERN ENGLAND TRAILS
A Northern Coast to Coast Walk
Backpacker's Britain
    Northern England
Hadrian's Wall Path
The Dales Way
The Pennine Way

NORTH EAST ENGLAND, YORKSHIRE DALES AND PENNINES
Great Mountain Days in the Pennines
Historic Walks in North Yorkshire

South Pennine Walks
St Oswald's Way and St Cuthbert's Way
The Cleveland Way and the Yorkshire Wolds Way
The North York Moors
The Reivers Way
The Teesdale Way
The Yorkshire Dales
    North and East
    South and West
Walking in County Durham
Walking in Northumberland
Walking in the North Pennines
Walks in Dales Country
Walks in the Yorkshire Dales
Walks on the North York Moors – Books 1 & 2

NORTH WEST ENGLAND AND THE ISLE OF MAN
Historic Walks in Cheshire
Isle of Man Coastal Path
The Isle of Man
The Lune Valley and Howgills
The Ribble Way
Walking in Cumbria's Eden Valley
Walking in Lancashire
Walking in the Forest of Bowland and Pendle
Walking on the West Pennine Moors
Walks in Lancashire Witch Country
Walks in Ribble Country
Walks in Silverdale and Arnside
Walks in the Forest of Bowland

LAKE DISTRICT
Coniston Copper Mines
Great Mountain Days in the Lake District
Lake District Winter Climbs
Lakeland Fellranger
    The Central Fells
    The Far-Eastern Fells
    The Mid-Western Fells
    The Near Eastern Fells
    The Northern Fells
    The North-Western Fells
    The Southern Fells
    The Western Fells

Roads and Tracks of the
  Lake District
Rocky Rambler's Wild Walks
Scrambles in the Lake District
  North & South
Short Walks in Lakeland
  1 South Lakeland
  2 North Lakeland
  3 West Lakeland
The Cumbria Coastal Way
The Cumbria Way and the
  Allerdale Ramble
Tour of the Lake District

**DERBYSHIRE, PEAK DISTRICT
AND MIDLANDS**
High Peak Walks
Scrambles in the Dark Peak
The Star Family Walks
Walking in Derbyshire
White Peak Walks
  The Northern Dales
  The Southern Dales

SOUTHERN ENGLAND
Suffolk Coast & Heaths Walks
The Cotswold Way
The North Downs Way
The Peddars Way and Norfolk
  Coast Path
The Ridgeway National Trail
The South Downs Way
The South West Coast Path
The Thames Path
Walking in Berkshire
Walking in Essex
Walking in Kent
Walking in Norfolk
Walking in Sussex
Walking in the Cotswolds
Walking in the Isles of Scilly
Walking in the New Forest
Walking in the Thames Valley
Walking on Dartmoor
Walking on Guernsey
Walking on Jersey
Walking on the Isle of Wight
Walks in the South Downs
  National Park

WALES AND WELSH BORDERS
Backpacker's Britain – Wales
Glyndwr's Way
Great Mountain Days
  in Snowdonia

Hillwalking in Snowdonia
Hillwalking in Wales: 1&2
Offa's Dyke Path
Ridges of Snowdonia
Scrambles in Snowdonia
The Ascent of Snowdon
The Ceredigion and Snowdonia
  Coast Paths
Lleyn Peninsula Coastal Path
Pembrokeshire Coastal Path
The Severn Way
The Shropshire Hills
The Wye Valley Walk
Walking in Pembrokeshire
Walking in the Forest of Dean
Walking in the South
  Wales Valleys
Walking on Gower
Walking on the Brecon Beacons
Welsh Winter Climbs

**INTERNATIONAL CHALLENGES,
COLLECTIONS AND ACTIVITIES**
Canyoning
Europe's High Points
The Via Francigena
  (Canterbury to Rome): 1&2

EUROPEAN CYCLING
Cycle Touring in France
Cycle Touring in Ireland
Cycle Touring in Spain
Cycle Touring in Switzerland
Cycling in the French Alps
Cycling the Canal du Midi
Cycling the River Loire
The Danube Cycleway
The Grand Traverse of the
  Massif Central
The Rhine Cycle Route
The Way of St James

AFRICA
Climbing in the Moroccan
  Anti-Atlas
Kilimanjaro
Mountaineering in the Moroccan
  High Atlas
The High Atlas
Trekking in the Atlas Mountains
Walking in the Drakensberg

ALPS – CROSS-BORDER ROUTES
100 Hut Walks in the Alps
Across the Eastern Alps: E5

Alpine Points of View
Alpine Ski Mountaineering
  1 Western Alps
  2 Central and Eastern Alps
Chamonix to Zermatt
Snowshoeing
Tour of Mont Blanc
Tour of Monte Rosa
Tour of the Matterhorn
Trekking in the Alps
Trekking in the Silvretta and
  Rätikon Alps
Walking in the Alps
Walks and Treks in the
  Maritime Alps

**PYRENEES AND FRANCE/SPAIN
CROSS-BORDER ROUTES**
Rock Climbs in the Pyrenees
The GR10 Trail
The Mountains of Andorra
The Pyrenean Haute Route
The Pyrenees
The Way of St James
Through the Spanish Pyrenees:
  GR11
Walks and Climbs in the Pyrenees

AUSTRIA
The Adlerweg
Trekking in Austria's Hohe Tauern
Trekking in the Stubai Alps
Trekking in the Zillertal Alps
Walking in Austria

EASTERN EUROPE
The High Tatras
The Mountains of Romania
Walking in Bulgaria's
  National Parks
Walking in Hungary

FRANCE
Chamonix Mountain Adventures
Ecrins National Park
GR20: Corsica
Mont Blanc Walks
Mountain Adventures in
  the Maurienne
The Cathar Way
The GR5 Trail
The Robert Louis Stevenson Trail
Tour of the Oisans: The GR54
Tour of the Queyras
Tour of the Vanoise

Trekking in the Vosges and Jura
Vanoise Ski Touring
Via Ferratas of the French Alps
Walking in the Auvergne
Walking in the Cathar Region
Walking in the Cevennes
Walking in the Dordogne
Walking in the Haute Savoie
  North & South
Walking in the Languedoc
Walking in the Tarentaise and
  Beaufortain Alps
Walking on Corsica

GERMANY
Germany's Romantic Road
Hiking and Biking in the Black
  Forest
Walking in the Bavarian Alps
Walking the River Rhine Trail

HIMALAYA
Annapurna
Bhutan
Everest
Garhwal and Kumaon
Kangchenjunga
Langtang with Gosainkund
  and Helambu
Manaslu
The Mount Kailash Trek
Trekking in Ladakh
Trekking in the Himalaya

ICELAND & GREENLAND
Trekking in Greenland
Walking and Trekking in Iceland

IRELAND
Irish Coastal Walks
The Irish Coast to Coast Walk
The Mountains of Ireland

ITALY
Gran Paradiso
Sibillini National Park
Stelvio National Park
Shorter Walks in the Dolomites
Through the Italian Alps
Trekking in the Apennines
Trekking in the Dolomites
Via Ferratas of the Italian
  Dolomites: Vols 1 & 2
Walking in Abruzzo
Walking in Sardinia
Walking in Sicily

Walking in the Central
  Italian Alps
Walking in the Dolomites
Walking in Tuscany
Walking on the Amalfi Coast
Walking the Italian Lakes

MEDITERRANEAN
Jordan – Walks, Treks, Caves,
  Climbs and Canyons
The Ala Dag
The High Mountains of Crete
The Mountains of Greece
Treks and Climbs in Wadi Rum
Walking in Malta
Western Crete

NORTH AMERICA
British Columbia
The Grand Canyon
The John Muir Trail
The Pacific Crest Trail

SOUTH AMERICA
Aconcagua and the
  Southern Andes
Hiking and Biking Peru's
  Inca Trails
Torres del Paine

SCANDINAVIA
Walking in Norway

**SLOVENIA, CROATIA AND
MONTENEGRO**
The Julian Alps of Slovenia
The Mountains of Montenegro
Trekking in Slovenia
Walking in Croatia
Walking in Slovenia:
  The Karavanke

SPAIN AND PORTUGAL
Costa Blanca: West
Mountain Walking in
  Southern Catalunya
The Mountains of Central Spain
The Northern Caminos
Trekking through Mallorca
Walking in Madeira
Walking in Mallorca
Walking in Menorca
Walking in the Algarve
Walking in the Cordillera
  Cantabrica
Walking in the Sierra Nevada
Walking on Gran Canaria

Walking on La Gomera and
  El Hierro
Walking on La Palma
Walking on Tenerife
Walking the GR7 in Andalucia
Walks and Climbs in the
  Picos de Europa

SWITZERLAND
Alpine Pass Route
Canyoning in the Alps
Central Switzerland
The Bernese Alps
The Swiss Alps
Tour of the Jungfrau Region
Walking in the Valais
Walking in Ticino
Walks in the Engadine

TECHNIQUES
Geocaching in the UK
Indoor Climbing
Lightweight Camping
Map and Compass
Mountain Weather
Moveable Feasts
Outdoor Photography
Polar Exploration
Rock Climbing
Sport Climbing
The Book of the Bivvy
The Hillwalker's Guide to
  Mountaineering
The Hillwalker's Manual

MINI GUIDES
Alpine Flowers
Avalanche!
Navigating with a GPS
Navigation
Pocket First Aid and
  Wilderness Medicine
Snow

MOUNTAIN LITERATURE
8000m
A Walk in the Clouds
Unjustifiable Risk?

For full information on all
our guides, and to order
books and eBooks,
visit our website:
www.cicerone.co.uk.

Walking – Trekking – Mountaineering – Climbing – Cycling

Over 40 years, Cicerone have built up an outstanding collection of 300 guides, inspiring all sorts of amazing adventures.

Every guide comes from extensive exploration and research by our expert authors, all with a passion for their subjects. They are frequently praised, endorsed and used by clubs, instructors and outdoor organisations.

All our titles can now be bought as **e-books** and many as iPad and Kindle files and we will continue to make all our guides available for these and many other devices.

Our website shows any **new information** we've received since a book was published. Please do let us know if you find anything has changed, so that we can pass on the latest details. On our **website** you'll also find some great ideas and lots of information, including sample chapters, contents lists, reviews, articles and a photo gallery.

It's easy to keep in touch with what's going on at Cicerone, by getting our monthly **free e-newsletter**, which is full of offers, competitions, up-to-date information and topical articles. You can subscribe on our home page and also follow us on **Facebook** and **Twitter**, as well as our **blog**.

Cicerone – the very best guides for exploring the world.

CICERONE

2 Police Square Milnthorpe Cumbria LA7 7PY
Tel: 015395 62069 info@cicerone.co.uk
www.cicerone.co.uk